Voices in the Wilderness

Understanding the nature and authority of the true prophets of God

Kenyatta R. Arnette

KENYATTA R. ARNETTE, PHD
KRA Ministries, LLC

Voices in the Wilderness

To my mother who always supports my endeavors, believes
in all I dare to dream, and loves me into becoming

* * *

Voices in the Wilderness

Understanding the nature and authority of the true prophets of God

Later, I will give my Spirit to everyone.
Your sons and daughters will prophesy.
Your old men will have dreams,
and your young men will see visions.
In those days I will even give
my Spirit to my servants, both men and women.
Joel 2:28-29 (CEV)

Christ chose some of us to be apostles, prophets, missionaries, pastors, and teachers, so that his people would learn to serve, and his body would grow strong. This will continue until we are united by our faith and by our understanding of the Son of God. Then we will be mature, just as Christ is, and we will be completely like him.
Ephesians 4:11-12 (CEV)

Contents

Contents

Forward

Ephesians 4:11-16 (NIV)

[11] So Christ himself gave the apostles, the prophets, the evangelists, the pastors and teachers, [12] to equip his people for works of service, so that the body of Christ may be built up [13] until we all reach unity in the faith and in the knowledge of the Son of God and become mature, attaining to the whole measure of the fullness of Christ. [14] Then we will no longer be infants, tossed back and forth by the waves, and blown here and there by every wind of teaching and by the cunning and craftiness of people in their deceitful scheming. [15] Instead, speaking the truth in love, we will grow to become in every respect the mature body of him who is the head, that is, Christ. [16] From him the whole body, joined and held together by every supporting ligament, grows and builds itself up in love, as each part does its work.

In this wasteland of evangelical opportunity, empty spirituality, and rambunctiousness in the worship event, we must pose the provocative question, "Where are the true prophets of God?" All hell seems to have broken loose in the world and the faces and voices of the true prophets of God seems silenced and hidden behind the smokescreen of charismatic religiosity and prosperity teaching.

Something within you holds the reigns of your destiny. It must be, not only, awakened with you but stirred and agitated causing you to walk into the destiny of your spiritual being. Who others want and expect for you to be according to their selfish agendas may not be who God has spiritually purposed for you to be, or to become. Soul-shifting is not the changing of your church membership from one denomination or covering to another; it is the total realignment of your life in accordance with the will and purpose of God. It is uncomfortable, unnerving, uncertain and unpredictable, but it is necessary for your survival.

In authoring this book, I had to be placed in an awkward and uncomfortable place. It was a time of great uncertainty in which fear, and anxiety crippled the world as the COVID-19 pandemic spread worldwide. It was during this time that the Lord revealed that my isolation was to be a time of preparation, preparation for the next season in my life and ministry. While under "shelter-in-place orders," I surrendered to the unction of the Holy Spirit bidding me clearance to speak, "Son of God, speak in this season. Your time is now."

Having previously authored books, I was familiar with the process of developing an idea and then translating those thoughts into timeless literary wealth and value. That is not to say the previous works were masterpieces by any means. I understand the tedious nature of the writing process. It is evolutionary and discovery. Regardless of the errors in publication, the words on each page were infused with love and passion to empower others in this life of Christian ministry.

However, this experience harbored something profoundly different, the prophet within me was stirred and awakened. Previously, I found myself motivated to write based on life circumstances, obligations, and personal and professional time schedules. I faced degree completion, church conference deadlines, family life, relocation, and the confrontation with the terminal life expectancy of a loved one. Nevertheless, this time there was an unexplainable burning within consuming my inner man until it burst forth through the silence of isolation. It was during a period of isolation and global pandemic that divine revelation began to flow forth as a river of living water withheld by a dam of indecision and missed opportunities cresting at every waking moment until the mouth of the dam opened and life began to flow forth.

I heard the Spirit of the Lord speak unto me, "This is the season of My prophets. I am raising an army of prophets, generals in My army, commanders of the people, to sound forth the living word of the Lord to the church. Speak life. Speak hope. Speak correction. Speak My word and this people shall live again," declares the Lord. Lord, this prophet is listening and moving according to Your voice. More than anything we can see, touch, taste, or desire in our flesh, God needs willing vessels of God's glory to commune in God's presence to hear God's voice and then boldly declare to the world God's divine will, not the will or agendas that we have created and spoken falsely and selfishly to satisfy our own lusts for prestige, power, positions, and pleasure.

I opted to write in first-person because this is personal. I am vested in this work, and I am vested in you and in your becoming. Beloved, I am on divine assignment. When you are cognizant of divine assignment and divine appointment, your perspective and responsiveness change accordingly. Therefore, I am moving with purposeful intent and a sense of spiritual urgency.

Throughout this process, I was reminded on epiphanic moment in my ministry. More than a decade ago, I wrestled, like Jacob, with the Lord concerning my separation from the safety net of my traditional denominational affiliation. As God was calling me to greater responsibility and appointing me to intensified accountability, the Lord was simultaneously releasing me from that blanket of complacency under which I found myself. "Get up from here and go!" was the command.

Honestly, I could not understand why the Lord was shifting me from my place of comfort. The Lord uprooted me from all that was familiar into a barren wasteland of nothingness and nobody, no experience, no knowledge, no support, and no resources, and the list continues. In anger, I boldly questioned God, but in faith I humbly trusted God. Everything with God is with purpose and for a purpose. God's purpose may not always be clear, but the plan of God is always certain and sure.

Even though I no longer had those things that gave me confidence and security in ministry, a fine edifice, a definitive church appointment, and a guaranteed paycheck, I possessed all that I needed. It is in times of total dependence on God that your spiritual senses and awareness heighten. When the false evidence of faith has been removed, the power of God can be revealed and manifested in your life. As I look back at my experiences, in the absence of a denominational seal of approval, what I did have was the Spirit of God and an assignment from God.

In discovery and reflection, I realized that God removed me from the high place of denominational allegiance so God could deliver me into the prophetic vessel that I am becoming. God stripped me of haughty arrogance filling me with humble obedience, continual thirsting for more of God, more of God's Spirit, more is what I crave. I simply desire the more of God. Never satisfied and never satiated with what is; I simply seek God for more. What does God have next for me and my ministry? What more can I do? Who else can I reach? What doors will you open? God, what more?

Prior to departing my denomination, I consulted with a colleague in ministry. As I questioning and wrestling with God, she questioned me, "What has the Lord spoken to you? What has God spoken in your heart about your ministry?" My response was, "If I do not go, the Lord will hold me accountable. The blood of all those who must hear my voice and receive the message within me is upon me." That urgency has never died; it has been simmering and stirring quietly within. The blood of others is upon me. If I am not in position being used as the vessel I was divinely created to be, the souls of others may suffer potential loss because if I choose to abandon my position and calling.

You, like me, must fulfill your divine assignment. Your life, your ministry, your peace, your sanity, all that makes you who you are depends on you. Furthermore, the lives attached to your assignment depend on your fulfillment of your prophetic call. Whether you desire to or not, you must hear the prophet's call and act accordingly.

I am on a prophetic assignment to speak into the body of believers to help awaken the prophets which have lain dormant through the previous season of transition in the household of faith. You slept through earlier shifts in the Kingdom. You ignored the voice of God. You suppressed the power of God that was at work within you. You denied the calling God has on your life. You have compromised your spiritual thirst and hunger for the pleasures of the world, alcohol, sex, drugs, waywardness, disobedience, self-destructiveness, anything to please your physical body but denying your spiritual temple.

God has a word for you, "Get up from here and go!" In this season of abiding grace that you must act with haste and purposeful intention. You must take hold of that which God has designed for you, every talent, every gift, and every calling.

There are lives waiting on you. There are souls awaiting the sound authority of your voice and your witness. There are generations of prophets impregnated within you lying dormant awaiting their moment of birthing. God is summoning you to hear the prophet's call with your spiritual ears and respond within your heart and soul. The unction of God's anointing and purpose is upon you. Now is your season. Now is your time.

In my own becoming and awakening it has been my request that the Lord chastise my faith and the reluctance of my heart to stand in the watchtower of destiny to proclaim the unbridled prophetic voice of the Lord. Prophet of the Most-High God, come forth and take your place. Surrender your mind, body, and spirit to the power of God that you may become heaven's mouthpiece delivering words of life, hope, deliverance, and judgement to the people of God.

Every spiritual work begins and continues through prayer. We are commanded to always pray and to continuously exercise and live by our faith in God. In Luke 18, Jesus admonished his disciples of the importance and urgency of prayer. There is a multiplicity of reasons why we as believers, and nonbelievers alike, must pray. The resulting benefits of a sound life of prayer remain boundless.

We must never forget that prayer is the key to unlocking our under-standing of supernatural things. The people of God should pray for a myriad of reasons. We pray because it is our open line of communication with the spiritual realm through which we approach the Holy of Holies. We pray because through prayer we are strengthened from within the deepest reaches of our being. We pray because prayer is the critical aspect of the development our spiritual life and overall spiritual well-being. We pray as a means of activating divine resources and accessing spiritual help when we need it. We pray because it expedites divine authority in our situations enabling us to defeat and subdue every enemy which assails us, even the enemy within each of us.

Finally, through prayer we are empowered to access and release the Kingdom callings which lie dormant within us. Prayer is the arsenal of the Christian's power and authority. Without an active substantial prayer life, your witness is invalidated and your strength nonexistent. So, let us pray...

> Eternal God, bless those who read this work, those, who like me, find, and have found themselves going through life seeking full understanding of their purpose and their assignment. Grant to them divine wisdom, courage, direction, clarity of the vision, understanding of the purpose, knowledge of the plan, boldness to bear this mantle, and the authority to fulfill this assignment. Guide them by Your divine design. Release within them their Kingdom callings as prophets in this season and in this hour. Bring them into the place of divine calling, spiritual appointment, and destiny, extending themselves prostrate before You in Your Holy of Holies to receive a double portion of Your Spirit for the work ahead. It is in Your Holy Name I pray through Jesus our Christ.

> *Ashé*

Examine Yourself

2 Corinthians 13:3-5 (RSV)

³ Since you desire proof that Christ is speaking in me. He is not weak in dealing with you, but is powerful in you. ⁴ For he was crucified in weakness, but lives by the power of God. For we are weak in him, but in dealing with you we shall live with him by the power of God. ⁵ Examine yourselves, to see whether you are holding to your faith. Test yourselves. Do you not realize that Jesus Christ is in you?—unless indeed you fail to meet the test!

We need a true word from God, not mediocre rhetoric or the regurgitation of a myriad of cliches from oilless individuals. Oilless because they lack the fervor and anointing of God, ministering without a message and preaching without real power. No more sounding brass or clanging cymbals pretending and perpetrating to possess the authority which can only obtained from the purging of flaming coals on the altar of God found only within the holy of holies, a place only few have been chosen to enter.

The hour of impotent prophets spreading empty messages to glorify themselves and to draw the attention of people to themselves has ended. God and the salvation of humanity and God's church demands the resurgence of the true prophets od God, not ego-hungry attention-seeking opportunist. The prophetic work demands deep unbridled intimate relationship with God and unity with the Holy Spirit. You must be ready and equipped for the warfare that awaits you in this spiritually compromised world. Even the church has been compromised.

As I pondered the mounting challenges which confront our faith, I was reminded of a text in Judges 19, a very painful, dark, and gloomy biblical text, yet very pungent and relevant for our time as we consider the issues contained within this text, as well as those of our present time. The text opens the first verse with the realization of the absence of true spiritual leadership, "And it came to pass in those days, when there was no king in Israel," and then the chapter closes with this staggering demand, "Just imagine! We must do something! So, speak up!"

Whether we are prepared to acknowledge it or not, the pulpit has a duty to speak up and to speak out. Those called to prophetic ministry have not been called to negotiate automobile and real estate loans or to play matchmaker to those searching for love. Our duty is to speak up and to speak out concerning the human condition and those things concerning the Spirit of God. We must condemn what must be condemned and speak life where life needs to happen. God requires such boldness in prophets. We have an obligation to God and to the people that we serve to speak up and to speak out, but you must ask yourself the question, "Am I the one God is calling for in this season? Am I ready and equipped for the work of the prophet?"

Let us be clear, transparent, and honest; there is nothing so amazingly wonderful about you that God should call or need you to do God's work. Who do you think you are that God would call or consider you, the mess that you are and with all that you have done? A prophet? God's spokesperson? Why you? Why not you? It is the mere fact that you are who you are which justifies your elevation and appointment.

Psalm 115:12-13 (RSV)

[12] The Lord has been mindful of us; he will bless us; he will bless the house of Israel; he will bless the house of Aaron.

[13] He will bless those who fear the Lord, both small and great.

God sees and knows us and will be faithful to bless us regardless of who we are. God sees and knows all and speaks into our human situations rhema messages. In seasons of success, joy, and gladness, God speaks. But it is our same caring, compassionate, covenant-making God, who in times of confusion and trouble, God speaks. Amidst chaos and confusion, God speaks. Even during our melancholy journey through the valley of the shadow of death, God speaks. It is through the voices and mouths of tried and trusted prophets that "The Invisible God" has continued to speak and convey the complexities and intricacies of the divine plan.

Are you that voice? Are you the voice prepared, tried, and trusted to carry and proclaim to the world as the mouthpiece of God? While God is speaking throughout the heavens, who among us is speaking for God declaring to the people all that God has spoken making clear the plan of God before the congregations of the earth?

Where are the true prophets of our time? Are there any true prophets remaining in the land? We must ponder this question, who will speak on God's behalf, or has God ceased speaking just as God did during the near four hundred years between the Old and New Testaments known as the "Dark Ages"? God is speaking but we cannot hear God because of the constant noise and clamoring of life which include technological accessibility, social media influences, political dissension and discourse, religious rhetoric, pandemic outcomes, and the prevalence of social injustice around the world.

If the church and the people of God are to overcome and survive, we need God to move as never before. We need God to break the silence of heaven and shatter the darkness of our present situations with an unleashed word, a fresh rhema word, to heal the spiritually wounded and exercise the darkness and spiritually wicked among us. The Church Universal needs to bombard heaven, "Lord, send us true prophets to speak on Your behalf. Send us anointed vessels, those oracles endowed with spiritual wisdom and insight to reveal Your truths to us and the certainty of Your presence among us."

We need bona fide prophets to boldly proclaim God's message throughout this wilderness we call life. The Bible commands us to examine ourselves and to be self-reflective in the process of seeking and securing the purity of holiness. Holiness the way of life for the chosen of God. Before you begin declaring yourself a "prophet" you had better check yourself before you find yourself wrecked upon the journey.

Repeating a bunch of Bible verses and clichés does not make you a prophet any more than sharing obvious good news with others. Just because you made a statement which seemed to have happened does not make you a prophet. Prophesying is the divine spiritual act of becoming the very vessel through and by which The Eternal speaks into time and space. It is fresh, relevant, revelation about the awesomeness of God in our time.

Prophets have a place in the life every believer for they speak to our everyday situations as God would deem necessary for the situations in which we find ourselves. Every word professed to have prophetic authority is not prophetic; other statements are simply obvious and determined through observation and speculation. The true prophet of God must hear beyond what they hear in the natural and see beyond what they see in the realm of the physical. Prophets are the timeless revealers of divine truth.

Divine prophecy comes during seasons of chaos, calamity, confusion, and uncertainty. God speaks to resolve and rectify our issues and to deliver us assurance and hope in uncertain times. Prophecy speaks to situations and conditions. It is not random or generalized but sent to a particular person/people for a specific purpose. Prophetic revelation is purposeful and intentional.

The prophet is the voice of God in this present hour and for this season. Pity the prophet who lacks spiritual vision and insight into the mind of God. They must know God and be in relationship with God possessing sound theological understanding of who God is. Because of the depth of God's knowledge and love for humanity and God's concern for the human condition, we must release ourselves from minimalistic thought processes concerning the person and nature of God and what God can accomplish in the lives of humanity.

Believers beware! It is not the work of the prophet to perform, fulfill, or manifest the actuality of a divine promise. It is the work and responsibility of the prophet to pronounce and proclaim the promises of God in the lives of God's people and before nations and kingdoms, with definitive certainty and clarity. Prophets must remain before the Lord and in the face of God with their ears and hearts attuned to the voice of the Lord. Prophets must have something to say from God. Reciting clichés, anecdotes, Bible verses, and religious rhetoric does not assure prophetic authority.

Prophets share with an assigned people that which God has spoken to them through dreams, visions, whispers, and spiritual unction. Prophets reveal and speak the mysteries of Spirit of God. The people will question. They will seek validation and assurance. People will question and challenge your authority as a prophet of God. It behooves every prophet to seek from God a clear understanding of the message being conveyed and to be certain of the words spoken. Once spoken, you cannot retract what has been stated. You are accountable for your words.

Undeniably, this work is indeed divine. Unlike any other vocation, calling, assignment, appointment, or affiliation, the prophetic work requires the fullness and totality of you. It demands the full engagement of your whole self. It is such that the Spirit of God seeks in this season. Unless you are prepared to take an introspective journey into the abyss of your experiences intimately exploring your strengths, weaknesses, shortcomings, desires, flaws, and fallacies; unless you are prepared to confront and expose all of who you are, you are not fit for the prophetic assignment.

The magnitude of the prophetic assignment is unequivocally and uniquely different. It transcends our deepest desires and fears. This is a spiritual undertaking which cannot be confused with works of the flesh or things comprehended through our physical senses. The mantle of the prophet surpasses our utmost aspirations, dreams, and hopes forging into realms of the unknown.

Our world and faith are suffering due to the absence of prophetic witness, not prosperity pushing, but true prophetic unction to speak to the evils of this world, the principalities, powers, and spiritual wickedness found in high places. The prophets of God must stand boldly and confidently upon the words of the Apostle Paul found in 2 Corinthians,

2 Corinthians 10:3-6 (RSV)

[3] For though we live in the world we are not carrying on a worldly war,

[4] for the weapons of our warfare are not worldly but have divine power to destroy strongholds.

[5] We destroy arguments and every proud obstacle to the knowledge of God, and take every thought captive to obey Christ,

[6] being ready to punish every disobedience, when your obedience is complete.

As a prophet of the Lord, you are a human weapon of the destruction and decimation of evil in the world, not a conjurer of good fortune, material acquisitions or wealth, or healthy love lives. This calling and assignment are more than that and demand more.

Prophetic work exists as a marriage between the individual and the Spirit of God to function in a oneness for the edification of God's people, the glorification of God, and the destruction of forces of darkness. Strongholds and curses must be destroyed. The prophet's sole work is to reveal God's truth in a dark and dying world to fulfill the purposes of God, not to please the ears and hearts of individuals. As prophet, you are God's spokesperson, not the people's champion.

It must be made clear though, the marriage of the individual with the Spirit of God does not make the human vessel of equal status or importance with the Spirit. As the vessel through which spiritual revelations are shared, you have no priority in this work. The work and the focus are not about you; you are not the central focus of the prophetic venture. When you become the central focus of your ministry, you have abandoned the marriage with the Spirit. You are merely the conduit by which and through which God speaks to the world; by which God delivers us from darkness; by which God heals all manner of illnesses and diseases, and by which God sets people free from the bondages of this world. It is through you, not of or about you, that the work takes place.

Those who engage in prophetic ministry must become transparent with themselves. The work will require them to reveal the deepest depths of who they are, their experiences, their desires, their fears, their dreams, their aspirations, their prejudices, their dislikes, their flaws, and even their hopes. All these are aspects of who you are; all of this must be revealed and exposed so God can use you in the fullness of who you are as God's prophet.

There can be no hidden agenda between the prophet and the One who calls and anoints prophets for the work we do. It does matter to God if you, like Noah, still crave the consumption of alcohol, or if, like David, your proclivity for sexual gratification consumes you. It matters not to God if you, like Moses, bear the burden of a physical disability or impairment which heightens your insecurities or thoughts of inadequacy for the work ahead. It does not matter if you, like Paul, have spent your years harboring hatred toward others, or have lived so critical of others because of your allegiance to unorthodox traditions and religiosity. You could be like Abraham hearing the voice of God and knowing the promises of God for your life but find yourself consumed with your own agenda and attempts to make God's promises happen.

Beloved, allow God to fulfill God's plan. Abandon that spirit of defiance and obey God's commands to reap God's promised blessings. You could be like Job, too reliant on the opinions of your friends and preoccupied with the opinions of others concerning you. Sometimes the opinions of others may cause you to waver in your position and assignment in God's Kingdom.

Beloved, God knows you and knows all about you. Regardless of your background, your issues, reservations, or fears, when God peers through time and space and sees the potential of your future divine promises take shape and form. God will perform God's best work in you. God will use you and all your shortcomings to accomplish significant work for God in the deliverance, redemption, and salvation of God's people.

God has prepared and equipped you for the work which lies ahead. Your shortcomings, fallacies, flaws, errors, and mistakes have undergirded you with wisdom, imbued you with strength, and equipped you with a firm foundation for prophetic ministry. Your life experiences provide you with an understanding of the human condition which is the foundation upon which your ministry will evolve and develop. An awareness and sincere appreciation for the general human condition, the complexities of the situations in which we find ourselves in life, in addition to the host of challenges which confront our humanity will equip the prophet with the greatest power of all as prophets – genuine loving compassion.

Compassion is the ability to sympathize and show genuine concern for the situations of others. Ministry without compassion is pointless and meaningless. All that God does for us is because God cares for us. How dare you attempt to speak on God's behalf or serve as ambassadors of heaven yet lack genuine interest in or concern for those whom God loves. True compassion empowers every prophet and to brings credibility to the words we speak, thus allowing us to minister effectively to people who are like us, flawed, tattered, wounded, and broken. Compassion for the world led Christ to the cross. Unconditional love for all held him on the cross.

You must inquire of yourself, "Why am I doing this?" You assess your motives and evaluate your own actions and wonder, "What is your purpose for doing this type of ministry?" Being a prophet can be lonely and thankless; it is not glorious; it is not popular; it is self-less giving of yourself. Examine yourself. Why are you here? What are you going to do with that which God has deposited and entrusted to you?

{ 2 }

It Begins with Your Yes

2 Corinthians 1:17-22

[17] Was I vacillating when I wanted to do this? Do I make my plans like a worldly man, ready to say Yes and No at once? [18] As surely as God is faithful, our word to you has not been Yes and No. [19] For the Son of God, Jesus Christ, whom we preached among you, Silva'nus and Timothy and I, was not Yes and No; but in him it is always Yes. [20] For all the promises of God find their Yes in him. That is why we utter the Amen through him, to the glory of God. [21] But it is God who establishes us with you in Christ, and has commissioned us; [22] he has put his seal upon us and given us his Spirit in our hearts as a guarantee.

Humble submission to authority is a perquisite for prophetic ministry. The temptation to vaunt oneself looms over the life of the prophet. However, the prophetic office is not about the individual; this ministry centralizes its message and efforts on God and God's movement among humanity. You must suppress any notion which impedes your willingness to totally submit and surrender to God.

Not only must you submit to the will of God, but an authentic prophet submits also to pastoral leadership for guidance, spiritual nurturing, and support. I have witnessed the shift in the prophetic office from responsibility and accountability to unruly behavior, rambunctious disposition, careless interactions, and spiritual apathy. You cannot be God's prophet and not be willing or able to submit to leadership and governance over you. Our God is one of order and decency. Chaos and disorder are the antitheses of the nature of God. When you refuse to submit to order, your prophetic mantle has shifted from a holy anointing to an obsessive demonic objectivity.

As a herald of divine truth, an orator of hope, and a prognosticator of peace, the prophet must remain ready to pronounce God's word, will, wrath and judgement, without reservation, dispense and proclaim divine blessings, as well as wield God's rod of correction. You must be endued with the proclivity for truth and justice at any cost. Prophets, however, are not above reproach, chastisement, or correction. The word of God has a double edge, and thus as boldly as you deliver it you must receive it.

The work of the prophet begins with your, "Yes!" This is not a "yes" to popularity or favor with the masses, but yes to a life of intentional devotion, introspective reconciliation, independent prognostication, inadvertent misunderstandings, and isolated servitude. You will serve God in total dependence upon the Lord alone yet receiving inexplicable rewards through your faith in God.

Begin to see yourself as more than your past experiences, more than the circumstances through which you have overcome, more than the obstacles over which you have triumphed, and more than the negative criticisms of your personhood which you have had to transcend. You are more than the mistakes you have made and more than the flaws that you bear. You are as God sees you. You are as God has created you. And you shall accomplish what God has purposed.

What is transpiring within you is transformation. God has begun the process of shifting your purpose to align it with your destiny. Externally you appear the same; you look the same and you are indeed the same person you have been. However, change is taking place within you, shaping you, growing you, elevating you, transforming you. Your spiritual thirst, zeal, and insight have begun to intensify causing you to question yourself, and in other cases, you may have doubt or reservations about what it is you are hearing or seeing. Beloved, you are being transformed, not by the renewing of your mind, but you have been rebirthed for renewal of your mind and your spirit to equip you for this most unexpected journey.

Until your soul says "Yes," your gift and your calling will never manifest. While remain paralyzed with fear abandoning the calling upon your life, too many undeserving have become part of the proliferation of the uncalled, unanointed, and unappointed, self-proclaimed prophets in the church. Until you surrender to the unseen power working within you (creating, living, breathing, saving, healing, molding, making, shaping, holding, forming, embracing, reviving, restoring...working), and hearken to that voice calling you, your destiny will remain beyond your reach and grasp. The Lord's sheep know the voice of their Lord and they respond and heed God's call with an obedient spirit.

Your divine appointment through the unction of the Holy Spirit to fulfill the duties of a spiritual office commences at your proclamation. When you say "Yes" to the Lord, God releases that which will be needed to walk ministry. Before you profess to prognosticate on God's behalf, you must emphatically proclaim, "Yes," from the deepest recesses of your soul and being as you surrender your life and will to the uncompromising authority of Holy Spirit.

Proclamation of this magnitude is more than spouting forth cliches, reciting memorized scriptures, or delivering empty promises to rouse the pockets and purses of trusting individuals. The prophetic office demands that you declare with utmost and unwavering certainty, assurance, and authority the positive acknowledgement, affirmation, and acceptance of the unknown uncertainties which accompany the assignment of God which lies ahead of you. Up until now, you have seen and decided based upon what you see, but for this journey, your faith in God must do the seeing for you as you trust and rely on God. Beloved, it begins with your, "Yes."

Nothing that I can say in this book will have any merit or meaning until you say, "Yes" to God and the call upon your life and the weight of the tasks that lie ahead of you. You can do and think what you will, but the wealth and value of what is to be shared will have greater meaning once you give God your "Yes." The work begins with your response of faith to God's calling and appointment to the office of a prophet. This is not a work for those who thirst for power, prestige, or position, but it yields to those who truly hunger and thirst for the righteousness of God and who seek humble submission to the threshing floor of the Holy One, those whose lips have been purged by the flaming coals of God's altar.

So much is now said about the ways of the "old church." Unfortunately, things spoken have been spoken in condemnation of the historic practices, polities, and policies which have carried and sustained us as a people through the darkest and most desolate periods in our history. This is not to say that the church is, or was, perfect in any way. The need for cognitive, intellectual, and spiritual growth remains undeniable and drastically needed to advance the church and the people of God to the next level. Nevertheless, we must admit that there were fundamental practices which positioned the church in a spiritual position to overcome the oppressions and abuses which befell marginalized communities, especially the African American community with reference to the implications of centuries of racism, slavery, discrimination, and injustice. It was the simplistic faith in God that was taught, learned, and practiced in the "old church" which enabled us to travail through hurt, hardships, and heartache to achieve and accomplish that which we as a people have.

While there are acts and traditions of the "old church" should remain treasures of the past, conversational pieces, foundational stones of our Zion, other traditions must remain alive to maintain the fervor and power of the church in this new modern church experience.

Bearing this in mind, I am drawn immediately to the unwavering faith of the people in the power of God to do the impossible. The "old church" was comprised of people with limited education and resources, they had no access to advanced technology or electronic devices such as cell phones, tablets, smart watches, and so much more. Yet, these were people who exhibited an undeniable right now kind of faith, and nothing they experienced or encountered was able to break or shake their faith.

Faith. It is the power that makes the difference and changes things and people despite the obvious or ostentatious.

Faith. It is the foundation upon which our destinies have been established.

Faith. It is the activity of the human heart in an undying quest for divine manifestations and supernatural movements in our time.

Faith. It moves mountains. It calms stormy seas. It causes the possible to arise from the depths of the deepest impossibility.

Faith. It is the evidentiary proof and provisional gratification of the very things for which we have hoped and prayed.

If you are to fulfill your destiny then who you are in God, how you operate, and the work to which you have been called cannot function in the absence of faith in God. The possession and exercise of faith is the solitary requirement for bringing pleasure to God. Trying to operate without faith is like attempting to operate an automobile without the very element which fuels its movement and performance. You must have faith.

Fear is the antithesis and nemesis of faith. It opposes faith. Fear impedes and impairs the boldness and assurance of our movement forward. Fear is rooted in what we see and perceive. This journey is a walk of faith, not one dependent upon what we see. You cannot walk in the fear of the unknown and walk in faith simultaneously. You must make the conscious choice to follow the plan of God. Faith is not about you, nor is it concentrated on your abilities or efforts to perform any miraculous feat. True faith is the epitome of a "God-moment;" God remains both subject and object.

Faith is not just believing but also trusting wholeheartedly. Faith says to God, "I do not see, know, comprehend, or conceive what lies ahead, nor how or why it will happen in my life, but I trust You and I trust your plan that all will be well and that all things will work for my good." The prophet of God must walk and operate in unbridled faith in the power, presence, potential, and purpose of God's plan. It is the utmost requirement of our spiritual servitude.

From every prophet, those called and appointed by God to speak and serve as Heaven's oracle, the very mouthpiece of the Divine, God requires your "Yes." In the tradition of the "old church," the faith of the individual believer was called upon and demanded as the church participated in what we called "Tarrying Service." Such services pulled upon the undying faith and hope of the people. Tarrying services were unscripted and lacked doctrinal order and the ritualistic practices of our human creation. During such services, people came seeking an encounter with God. Believers would call upon the Name of the Lord until the Heavens would open, and the power of God would descend.

It is believed that if you call God true and long enough, God will show up. Something would happen. The atmosphere would shift as heaven manifested itself within the physical sacred space. Such transcendent spiritual experiences must once again return to the house of God if the church is to regain its power and position throughout the world. Such services demanded our faith as we called collectively upon the Lord to move and a abide among us to ignite supernatural change within our situations to manifest the power of the Holy Spirit within us – transformation, deliverance, healing, miracles, blessings, and breakthroughs.

"Say, 'Jesus!'"

"Say, 'Jesus!'"

"Say, 'Jesus!'"

"Call Him!"

"Call Him until you feel Him moving within you."

"Jesus!"

"Jesus!"

"Jesus!"

Such callings of faith demanded the presence of God, and not just the presence but the outcome of our faith, the answer to our prayers, and the solutions to our every problem and concern. Such blind unquestionable faith must come alive in the church of today. It is the duty and responsibility of every prophet to awaken this faith within the body of believers. Such faith must be the power and hope of the prophetic voice.

We must have a "Yes" in our spirits and within our mouths. When God calls us to this work, it requires our faith in action. You do not know how God will use you, nor what assignment God has for you, but faith in God must produce a solid "Yes" to the calling, appointment, and the assignment. It is the energy and fervency of the faith found in the "old church" which must fuel the ministry of the prophets.

"Say, 'Yes!' to the Lord."

There is power in your "Yes."

There is healing in your "Yes."

The deliverance of God's people rests in your "Yes."

God is waiting on your "Yes."

The moment that you say, "Yes" will be the moment your life will change immediately and will cease to be your own. With every opportunity, the enemy will stand in opposition, but rest assured, the Lord is on your side and the arsenal of Heaven will be at your disposal as God uses you to speak words that will save, heal, deliver, destroy, set free, uproot, build up, and tear down. The fire of God's Kingdom rests within you.

Hear me and hear me well. Your "Yes" to the Lord is not about your approval of the appointment or the assignment. God does not need nor require you to approve or cosign the assignment; God merely demands the willingness and availability of your total being, your mind, body, and soul. In fact, most times, true prophets are filled with reluctance about the assignment because they sense the outcome awaiting the disobedient. The proclamation of "Yes" to the will and calling of God, is your oath of spiritual surrender to God's will and to God's divine plan. You are pledging your life to the service of the Lord and surrendering yourself to what God demands of you in the timing and purpose of God.

It is not about what you like, or what you think. Your "Yes" commits you to go where God sends you and to be used by God as God needs. Here is the benefit of saying yes to God. You commit your life, the totality of your being, with the full understanding that whatever you need to effectively and impactfully fulfill your assignments, as God did for Abraham on the mountainside, God will provide. Do yourself a favor and remove yourself from the equation of your decision making. This journey is not about you. It simply requires your willingness.

The voice of the modern prophet is needed to propel the church into its newest dimension. This new dispensation of the Holy Spirit demands the "yes" of those willing to be sanctified, not as conformity to a denominational polity, but in full surrender to the will and power of God and so to be transformed as God deems and used as God wills. Yes, is the confirmation of your heart and soul. It is the submission of your individual will to the greater will of God. It is the denouncement of continued purposeful distrust, denial, and disobedience to God. It is trusting God with the impossibilities of life.

Growing in Your Season

2 Peter 3:14-18 (RSV)

[14] Therefore, beloved, since you wait for these, be zealous to be found by him without spot or blemish, and at peace. [15] And count the forbearance of our Lord as salvation. So also our beloved brother Paul wrote to you according to the wisdom given him, [16] speaking of this as he does in all his letters. There are some things in them hard to understand, which the ignorant and unstable twist to their own destruction, as they do the other scriptures. [17] You therefore, beloved, knowing this beforehand, beware lest you be carried away with the error of lawless men and lose your own stability. [18] But grow in the grace and knowledge of our Lord and Savior Jesus Christ. To him be the glory both now and to the day of eternity. Amen.

The decision to grow is your choice. What you want out of life and of your ministry is a conscious decision you must make. No one can make you do it, only you have the power to do it. You can choose to grow, or you can succumb to the pressures of ministry and die amidst your struggles.

You must determine within yourself that you want to grow and then position yourself in fertile territory. Your success is your responsibility. Align yourself with spiritual people who are also committed to growing and succeeding in ministry, those determined to transform the world, not those being transformed by the world. Attach and affiliate with spiritual resources which will add value to your ministry, not devalue or diminish the quality, mission, focus, or integrity of your ministry, or you for that matter. The spiritual attachments that you make in ministry should never lead you to compromising who you are to gain acceptance, acknowledgement, or affirmation. Those around you and connected to you should aid and encourage you to grow.

Like plants, flowers, and trees, you must grow in the direction of the sun (Son). Each of us must possess within us the desperation to grow and thrive, not by means of compromise of through the slandering and destruction of the character of others. Growth in ministry, and personally, can and will only come as you intentionally and purposefully seek the light of the sun. Despite the darkness, devastation, and dismay, or any other obstructions you may encounter, grow in the direction of the sun's (Son's) compassionate warm embrace. It is within the rays and reach of the sun (Son) that you will find safety and receive the nourishment and the strength needed to grow in your season.

Growth and maturity take time; they do not occur overnight. Wisdom demands that you seize every opportunity to become better; to hone your craft; to master your call; to perfect your spiritual giftings; to grow into your divine greatness. Growth is the natural action of every living thing from the moment of conception, even to the moment of death, life continues to grow and transform from one state of being into another form of life energy. In life, we are innately equipped with the tolls and abilities to reproduce after our own kind thus continuing the process of life by giving life. Producing and reproducing that which is useful and which aids in the betterment, continuance, and furthering of life is the purpose of every living thing.

Growth requires the embodiment of wisdom; not the futile and finite wisdom of ourselves and our situations, but wisdom of the divine and that which transcends ourselves because life is greater than our mere existence. Therefore, we must move and operate from the place of divine wisdom, not from the shadows of selfish ambition or through the selfish abandonment of our calling and our purpose. We owe it to ourselves, those who came before us, and those who shall come after us to engage in life with the understanding of who we are in God and how we see and comprehend God living and thriving within us transforming us into a greatness destined to be used for a greater purpose.

Wisdom, beloved, is our needed and valued guide. In fact, her handiwork orchestrates and charters the course of life for all living beings. It was in wisdom that King Solomon penned the immortal messages contained within the Book of Ecclesiastes, and so, consider these words,

Ecclesiastes 3:1,11-12 (NIV)

[1] There is a time for everything, and a season for every activity under the heavens...

[11] He has made everything beautiful in its time. He has also set eternity in the human heart; yet no one can fathom what God has done from beginning to end.

[12] I know that there is nothing better for people than to be happy and to do good while they live.

Life is a gathering of seasons, good seasons, and bad seasons, happy and sad, sowing and reaping, walking, and fainting, prospering, and sacrificing, smiling, and crying, living, and dying. Seasons, whatever they are, come and go. However, the good news is that no season, not even the worst of seasons, lasts forever.

The hardest lesson we must learn to embrace in life is that life just happens. How and why life happens the way it does has nothing to do with who you are or what you have done to deserve it. However, it has everything to do with who you become and the greatness of your becoming.

I remember hearing my late pastor say, "Into every life, some rain must fall." No truer words have ever been spoken. In fact, I, like you have not only experienced the rain, but I have survived the deluge, the overwhelming flood of problems, pains, pressures, and predicaments. Whoever said life would be easy neglected to disclose the truth about life. In fact, whoever promised that troubles would be over has dismissed the truth of reality and have missed the opportunity to walk in my shoes. But despite what we have experienced, we must remain mindful of the words of promise, spoken to the Prophet Isaiah,

Isaiah 43:2 (NRSV)

> When you pass through the waters, I will be with you; and through the rivers, they shall not overwhelm you; when you walk through fire you shall not be burned, and the flame shall not consume you.

We have been through, and we will go through; yes, even you will go through. Despite your anointing and giftedness, you, too, will go through for the sake of your calling and your appointment. It is trying of your faith that will perfect your witness. Beloved laborer of Christ, no matter how hard the test nor how heated the furnace of our persecution we must never forget that the power of God continues to sustain and uphold us despite the circumstances and stress we endure. As God continues to develop you, and this process is an ongoing process continually evolving as God has need of us, you will become a witness to the words that, "God is with us." The level and intensity of intimacy with God will increase as Emmanuel becomes more personal to you and in your ministry. There can be no hidden agendas and secrecy between you and God whom you declare has called and anointed you for this work. You must grow in your relationship from secrets to full surrender.

My best description of life is that life, with its multifaceted dynamics and complexities metaphorically mimics an orchestral masterpiece of infinite possibilities harmonizing around the melody of one's divine purpose. Life is like that; each experience and episode our lives play a distinctively different tune. Although different in composition, each is banded together and united as a symphonic expression of whom God has called and anointed for you to be on life's journey. Your story is your story, and no one can fully understand the glory God delivers through you.

Our lives are comprised of a plethora of experiences, good and not so good experiences. There are days of sunshine, and days when storms assail. There are days and seasons when the winds blow, the waves roll, the breakers dash, the lightning flashes, and the thunder rolls. However, there are also seasons of peaceful valleys, calming waters, gentle breezes, and overwhelming sunshine. Life is full of the uncertain and the unexpected.

No such manual exists which detailing with exact precision the whole truth about life or the reality of life's seasons. Wisdom teaches us that we must embrace the seasons in which we find ourselves. For in embracing the fullness of our seasons we thus access the overwhelming power and potential which has been divinely reserved for each of us. I passionately believe that what we need and seek to succeed through life's journey, God has already prepared and provided for us. However, it behooves us to know the season, embrace the season, and reap from each season that which has been divinely aligned for us.

How do you deal with the seasons? How do you effectively manage the changing of seasons? How do you deal with the truth of life and all that it entails, the ups, the downs, the celebrations, the sadness, the sorrow, the happiness, the hurts, the heartache, the triumphs, the troubles, tests, the trials, the tears, the turmoil, the tragedies...the truth?

The challenge which awaits each of us is learning to live after the storms have ceased. After everything has fallen apart and your life has been dismantled from the core, life must go on. Whenever something life-altering occurs in my I always ask myself the question, "What are you going to do when tomorrow comes?" Unfortunately, the circumstances that we face are laced with such pain and laden with burdens which creates the extreme difficulty of seeing life beyond our present situations. The reality that we must face is that life and living remain before us despite the present predicaments which plague our existence.

There are days and hours in which the sun sheds light upon the path before us. But there are also days when the darkness is so deep that it appears to ebb away the joys of life and living as we are encompassed all around within its cold grip. Beyond the days and hours remain those moments when hope remains unseen, love remains unfelt, and peace unknown. There are days when the emotions may overwhelm and overtake you, feelings of joy mixed with sadness, contentment and fulfillment overshadowed with failure and disbelief, or sanity clouded by guilty and shame.

The struggles we encounter in life bear a similar characteristic of God in that God is no respecter of persons. Regardless of your social prowess or religious status, life has a way of attacking the very fibers of your psyche and destroying the character of your soul. Struggles have no preference. Circumstances arise. Life happens. Problems come and problems go. Nevertheless, life moves forward.

Despite what you experience, the good and the not so good, you have choices which must be made. Life can take you down. Problems may stagnate you. Predicaments may impair you. Situations may paralyze you. Or you can allow life to propel you into your purpose. You have the power and the authority to take what life delivers to you and to use that to elevate you. Life is your privilege. Living is your power. Choice is your divine authority.

There are those among you who would dare to declare, determine, and decide your path. No one, no person, has the authority to dictate or determine your destiny. Beloved, this is your season. You must decide who you be and how you will choose to live and thrive in your season. It behooves you to make the conscious decision of how you desire to overcome and transcend what life has presented before you. No one else can choose that for you. You are the one who walks in your shoes and the only one to captain your ship. Never surrender the authority of your destiny into the will of another.

What makes you and what shall determine how far you go and whom you evolve into being is determined by you. Your experience through life have merely presented various lenses through which you see the movement and mysteries of God unfolding in chaos of this world. No one has ever told you this but your experiences, all of them, whatever they may have been, were never intended to break, hurt, or crush you, or any of those other negative things (deflate, defeat, burden, dehumanize, discourage, destroy, belittle, berate, abuse, reject, neglect, and sabotage).

We have all felt the barrage of negative emotions at the expense of our peace and purpose along our journey. We have experienced those moments in which it seemed most appropriate to sever ourselves for others, life, our purpose, and our destiny. Each experience and every season have allowed you a different opportunity to experience and to encounter the Divine in a uniquely peculiar way, one which affords never-ending opportunities to fall in love with God, yourself, and life. Your experiences have been building you up for this season and this opportunity in life. Where you are going and what you are going to accomplish in this season far exceeds that which you have travailed and overcome.

Do not be afraid to live in your season. God has appointed such a time as this for you to do greater works. This a season in which you are to walk in the abundance of divine favor and opportunity. This is the season in which you shall speak fruitful things and see the manifestation of the words that you speak and the declarations that you decree. This is the season in which the words of the prophet will come to life taking shape and form in the lives of God's people.

It is by no accident that you are here, nor is it an accident that you hear. God is speaking to you so that God may speak through you. The season of your agenda has ended. Your push for prestige and positions has ended. God is calling forth prophets to speak spiritual truth to the powers of this world to free those who remain captive and bound to the ideological doctrines of spiritual disempowerment and allegiance to the wanton pleasures of self-gratification and entertainment which now plague the dwelling place of God.

Our misdeeds and failure to follow faith and reluctance to stand for God amidst the evil forces of this world have aroused God's attention. And do you know that God is not pleased. God is not pleased with our agendas. God is not pleased with our lackadaisical efforts to minister nor our proclivity to please people. God is not pleased with our lust for power or our fascination and enticement with indoctrinated vestments of impotent leadership.

God needs you. God sees you. God has anointed and appointed you for this season to do the work to build up and to tear down, to plant and to uproot. I hear the profoundly promising words of the Lord to the Prophet Joshua, "As I was with Moses, so shall I be with you."

God is with you so live and grow in your season. The season in which you now find yourself is not by happenstance. You are living, breathing, moving, and growing in this season because the Lord has deemed it to be so. God needs you in this season to grow into being – grow into your divine becoming. You don not fully comprehend who you are purposed to be in God's Kingdom. The plan of God for your life supersedes who you have been and what you have been through and all that you have assumed about yourself. What God is going to do through you in this season will surpass your greatest expectations, dreams, and desires.

The challenge that you now face as the elect of God is the acknowledgement of God's calling and appointment on your life. You must be willing to grow in this season and growing takes time, patience, and perseverance. You will not become great or master the dimensions of your calling overnight. You must have purpose and intention in all that you do and all that you say. The words you will speak will possess the power to transform lives, situations, circumstances, and outcomes. And your actions will have lasting consequences and implications which will impact the lives of countless souls.

Growing only begins when something has first been planted. Planting requires the presence of rich fertile ground, soil enriched with the nutrients which produce and yield a healthy and productive harvest. You cannot plant seeds or seedlings randomly or just anywhere; you must plant in ground that has been sufficiently tilled and prepared, ground free from the obstruction of weeds imitating true value and purpose yet constantly depleting the ground of its richness through the dissemination of poisonous toxins.

Beloved, your days, months, and years of wandering aimlessly through life and ministry must cease. You must be planted in the rich soil of endless possibilities, purpose, and assurance of hope in the eternal power of God. Anything that grows must be planted receiving vital nutrients from the soil which encompasses it. Not only must it be planted it must also be watered carefully and consistently receiving ongoing care to prevent it from dying from within.

What does all this mean? As one who has been called and appointed, you cannot meander without purpose. You must be planted and rooted deeply within ministry which nurtures, shelters, and provides richly for your continued growth, development, and sustenance. You must be willing to receive what is being delivered into you so that you may reciprocate and have value and wealth enough to deliver into others.

I pray that you grow and blossom in this season. It is my prayer that God position you in fertile fields of ministry which will nourish your calling and promote your growth, development, and elevation as God's prophet. It is my prayer that you are surrounded and supported by those who see your potential and understand the calling now placed upon your life. Whatever you seek to accomplish in ministry, however far you seek to reach as God's prophet, rest assured knowing that God will provide. God has much for you to do. Beloved, you have seeds to sow, fruit to bear, and a harvest to reap. There are prophecies to render, souls to save, and lives to transform. Even now, God is growing within you.

{ 4 }

Passing the Mantle

2 Kings 2:11-14 (RSV)

[11] And as they still went on and talked, behold, a chariot of fire and horses of fire separated the two of them. And Eli'jah went up by a whirlwind into heaven. [12] And Eli'sha saw it and he cried, "My father, my father! the chariots of Israel and its horsemen!" And he saw him no more. Then he took hold of his own clothes and rent them in two pieces. [13] And he took up the mantle of Eli'jah that had fallen from him, and went back and stood on the bank of the Jordan. [14] Then he took the mantle of Eli'jah that had fallen from him, and struck the water, saying, "Where is the Lord, the God of Eli'jah?" And when he had struck the water, the water was parted to the one side and to the other; and Eli'sha went over.

The prophetic assignment is weighted and heavy with divine purpose. It is costly in personal sacrifices of personal pleasures. However, it rewards those who faithfully commit to the calling and assignment. If a prophet is who you are, then prophesying is what you have been divinely anointed, appointed, and commissioned to do. It is incumbent upon the prophet to know and understand the assignment. And it behooves those who bear the assignment to consider the weighted expectation which has been divinely thrust upon the shoulders of the assigned.

There is a heaviness which rests on those in ministry. This assignment holds its strength and resilience in the promise made in the Psalms which indicates the multiplicity of afflictions which befall the righteous which shall continue to be overcome because of the abiding presence and authority of the Lord who remains on the side of the righteous (Psalm 34:19). Stand confidently upon the promises that you shall overcome and that it, whatever it may be in your life, shall happen.

I passionately believe that the Lord, who is our righteousness, endows us with an arsenal of internal strength which wells up within us in times of need to empower. Such strength and power come to propel us forward, catapulting us ahead of the potential destructiveness and devastation of our pain, and through every obstacle, setback, circumstance, crisis, and disturbance encountered along the journey. As God's prophet, you have God's ear and God's heart. Therefore, the heaviness of the assignment shall not prevail or overtake the prophet because your strength as God's prophet lies in the soundness and intimacy of your relationship with God. Every prophet must become deeply entangled and enmeshed in the presence of God and reliant upon the Spirit of God and not succumb to the temptation of self-reliance or pride.

It is not the heaviness of inexperience or the inability to fulfill one's assignment that challenges us the most. It is the heaviness of responsibility and accountability of knowing, understanding, and embracing your assignment. The work which God assigns to you may lead you into undesirably dark and desolate places: Lodebar, Nineveh, Patmos, Mount Seir, Damascus, Gadara, Samaria, Moab, Babylon, Rome, Pharaoh's temple, Herod's Hall, the belly of a whale, the wilderness, and even Golgotha. Your assignment is to go.

Matthew 6:30-33 (RSV)

[30] But if God so clothes the grass of the field, which today is alive and tomorrow is thrown into the oven, will he not much more clothe you, O men of little faith?

[31] Therefore do not be anxious, saying, 'What shall we eat?' or 'What shall we drink?' or 'What shall we wear?'

[32] For the Gentiles seek all these things; and your heavenly Father knows that you need them all.

[33] But seek first his kingdom and his righteousness, and all these things shall be yours as well.

It is your spiritual duty and responsibility to go where God sends you to do the spiritual work that God has commanded for you to do. And as you go, take the name of the Lord (which remains the strong tower of the righteous) with you and speak as the Spirit of God delivers and deposits into you to deliver.

The assignment is heavy and oft times unfavorable. However, the mantle is heavy and most undeserving. It requires the exposing of one's innermost desires, hopes, dreams, reservations, criticisms, critiques, and fears. The reception of the mantle uncovers the who that you truly are. You do not choose it, it chooses you. The mantle peers through the filthiness of your desires, the hidden vicissitudes of your life, and the archived experiences of your spiritual struggles and battles, both your losses and wins. The mantle reaches through the darkness of your past and embraces the emergence of light radiating through the heart of the you God has sanctified and commissioned you to become. Although it is most undeserving, because we have all sinned and fallen flat and short of the glorious nature of God because of the humanness of our physical being, it remains most hopeful, promising, spiritually rewarding. The mantle sees and knows all that you are, yet God has chosen you for such a time as this.

The inquiring nature of our humanity seeks comprehensive understanding. From the dawning of time, humanity has remained in a quest for truth and understanding of the complexities of life and the world in which we live. We long for the understanding our purpose and place in the vastness of time. Moreover, the unveiling of truth is the mission of our ministry. Therefore, it behooves us to fully understand the meaning and importance of the mantle.

A mantle is weighted garment which serves as an additional layer of clothing providing covering and protection from external elements. A mantle is often referred to as a cloak or a cape. It is worn loosely over one's garments draped over the shoulders and flowing the full length and depth of one's height and stature. In ancient times, a mantle was made of animal fur which provided warmth and protection from the weather and elements. It was a custom-made garment. With the naked human eye, the mantle was nothing mystical. However, the mantle was a necessary garment and served multiple purposes.

One of the best stories in the Bible to present us with an understanding of a mantle is the story of the Prophets Elijah and Elisha found in 2 Kings, Chapter 2. In this text, the Prophet Elijah (the senior teacher) is preparing for his death and departure. Elisha (Elijah's contemporary, his student or disciple) is not yet willing or ready to let go of his teacher and he holds on to every waking moment not allowing Elijah out of his sight. I have been in this place, unyielding to the inevitable moving of God to release those I love and those who nurtured me through life and my ministry into the eternal realm from my physical presence. We must willingly release those we love and lose to death and allow them soar.

In times of bereavement, we are often reminded of the text about being absent from the physical body. Grief and sadness are real and unavoidable roads we must take in life. The story of Elijah and Elisha is about the acknowledgement and acceptance of death, dying, sadness, and grief. It also demands that we consider how we are to live after those that we love transition from life through the vehicle of death. Elisha was grieving his pastor and teacher. This is a perspective often overlooked in the text. The text grapples with the reality of how we who are alive and remain live and move forward after those who birthed us and nurtured us have departed from us. Moreover, the transition of Elijah is about eternal authority and the possibilities of life through the transference of spiritual power.

An imperative lesson resides within the story of Elijah and Elisha. It is spiritually significant in understanding the importance of spiritual leadership in the growth, development, life, and death of ministry. Each generation of spiritual leaders must prepare and equip those who follow us with that which they will need to successfully navigate their way through the wilderness of ministry. Not only is true ministry about service to others but it equally demands preparation and empowerment of others to sustain the work and service with authenticity, truth, and legitimacy.

The relationship between Elijah and Elisha proves the importance of establishing and upholding a sound spiritual relationship between leaders and contemporaries. Boundaries, both spiritual and physical, are necessary and par for the journey. Far too many people ordain and consecrate individuals because of the hype of association and affiliation and the infatuation and the lust for power. People often seek offices of elevation out of vanity for vestments, not because they earnestly desire to do the laborious work of ministry. Spiritual legitimacy and integrity are missing in these relationships. Spiritual leaders must exert more discernment about whom they call and consider their children in ministry. Children in ministry are the direct reflection of those who imparted their hands upon them for the work of ministry. Likewise, the character and nature of a spiritual leader is embodied in the lives and ministries of those upon whom we ordain and consecrate. You must be extremely careful upon whom you lay hands.

Likewise, you must be equally concerned and discerning about those whom you allow to pray for you or cover you in spiritual authority. Stop choosing coverings, attachments, and affiliations based on superficial things such as how he/she looks, sounds, or makes you feel. Tap into the Spirit of God for guidance and discernment in matters of covering and elevation to offices of leadership in the church. It is imperative that we seek those who truly emulate and embody the Spirit of God, those who possess the heart of God for God's people, those who seek to do God's will sincerely and manifest the love of Christ, not the love of self or the desire for grandeur.

Character is critical in ministry. It is your defining glory, or it can end your story. There ought to be a sign displayed in every faith assembly which reads, "Beware: Spirits produce after their own kind." Our connections have much to do with who we become in ministry and who we produce through our ministry. A disobedient and contrary spirit will thus produce other likeminded spirits. A licentious spirit will thus produce licentious spirits. A whoremongering spirit will produce whoremongering spirits. You cannot ordain or consecrate individuals, then collect your fee and abandon and disown them because you failed to evaluate and investigate the character of such individuals, or you failed to equip and empower them with the defining character elements to distinguish them as worthy vessels of Christ and His calling.

Let me turn this around and give you the good news. When you are attached and nurtured by the right spirit and those who truly embrace and embody the light and love of God, it becomes evident in who you are and the ministry that you do. Like Elisha, who prayed for a "double portion" of his teacher's anointing, we ought to want to emulate and bring honor to the one who birthed us in the spirit of ministry. We should want to honor them through the works that we do and the lives that we live.

According to the story in the Old Testament Book of 2 Kings, even after his repeated warning of Elijah's impending departure, Elisha remained relentless in his commitment and attachment to Elijah and his teacher's presence. Beloved, as one who has been blessed to have my own "Elijah", a pastor who groomed and nurtured me taking me under her wing to prepare me for ministry, I understand Elisha's struggle. In our struggles to evolve and move forward in ministry, there are critical questions that we must ask ourselves. What am I reluctant to relinquish to God? What do I seek and expect from God? What is it that I fear? Do I honestly believe that God will deliver that which I seek? Read the following portion of the text.

2 Kings 2:9-15 (NKJV)

9 And so it was, when they had crossed over, that Elijah said to Elisha, "Ask! What may I do for you, before I am taken away from you?" Elisha said, "Please let a double portion of your spirit be upon me."

10 So he said, "You have asked a hard thing. *Nevertheless,* if you see me *when I am* taken from you, it shall be so for you; but if not, it shall not be *so.*"

11 Then it happened, as they continued on and talked, that suddenly a chariot of fire *appeared* with horses of fire and separated the two of them; and Elijah went up by a whirlwind into heaven.

12 And Elisha saw *it,* and he cried out, "My father, my father, the chariot of Israel and its horsemen!" So, he saw him no more. And he took hold of his own clothes and tore them into two pieces.

13 He also took up the mantle of Elijah that had fallen from him and went back and stood by the bank of the Jordan.

14 Then he took the mantle of Elijah that had fallen from him, and struck the water, and said, "Where *is* the Lord God of Elijah?" And when he also had struck the water, it was divided this way and that; and Elisha crossed over.

15 Now when the sons of the prophets who *were* from Jericho saw him, they said, "The spirit of Elijah rests on Elisha." And they came to meet him and bowed to the ground before him.

After reading this text, what do you feel? What did this text speak to you? What immediately grabs your attention?

Let me briefly focus on specific aspects of the text. Elisha had a clear understanding of his own spiritual expectations. He was tuned into spiritual self and his spiritual desires. Not only that but Elisha understood his purpose as a prophet and his desires and requests aligned with his purpose.

Furthermore, upon reading this text the inevitability and the inescapability of death plays a key role in the text. We must confront it as part of life's process. Death will come upon each of us like a flaming chariot pulled by swift horses. It will separate us from those whom we love and cherish in an instant. And like the flames of the chariot, the pangs of death can be felt as it leaves the evidence of its appearing singed upon our souls. The pain and reality of grief is real. Even for those in ministry, regardless of how deep and spiritually wonderful you think you are; death will shift you and cause you to respond in a host of ways. But it is healthy and necessary to release our anger and grief rather than internalize our pain perpetrating that we are stronger than we are. The good news is that there is an opportunity to live and to love after we grieve.

Notice, however, the unexpectedness of Elisha's deliverance. While he was grieving, God was blessing, and God was elevating. Prophets will experience loss. It is an unavoidable truth. We cannot desire the mantle spiritual ability of our parent in ministry yet refuse to release that person to God. Two cannot wear the same garment. You may have a garment like another, but two cannot simultaneously wear the same garment. In the fulness of time, when the early assignment of Elijah is concluded, God will release to Elijah's mantle that Elisha may then catch it and wear it.

Remember, the mantle is a weighted garment. It symbolizes the weight of responsibility and accountability to do the work of those who labored before and for you. Immediately, upon gathering himself and draping himself in Elijah's mantle, Elisha began to walk in the authority which had been given to him. It was evident and apparent even to those who later saw Elisha. They saw the spirit of their teacher Elijah resting now on the shoulders in the spiritual authority of Elisha.

Stop expecting fanfare and accolades from others. Prophetic ministry is not a popularity contest. Your effectiveness is not measured by your ability to rouse and hype up an audience of spiritually thirsty individuals. You are not called to be the prophet as means of income and personal gratification. You have been called to fulfill spiritual purpose and to bring others into the light and knowledge of their own destiny. You will speak with an authority that does not come from you. You are subject to the Holy Spirit; the Holy Spirit is not subject to you. You must submit to the Spirit; the Spirit does not submit to you. You must do the work and walk in the authority God has delivered to you. You cannot afford to grieve in your spirit over the loss of people, things, or opportunities forever. You must release the burden of our decisions and the weight of life's struggles and oppositions so that we can then shoulder the weight of ministry to bear full responsibility and accountability for the work waiting on you.

If Elisha grieved too long, destiny would have been delayed or denied. God needs you in your place of destiny because there are lives assigned to you, waiting on you. Stop waiting for things align according to your plan and your desires. The calling of God comes at a price which is the full surrender of your will to the divine will, care, and trust of God. This is a faith walk. You are the living example that we are not walking along this journey according to what we see in the natural. Your faith-sight will sharpen to more you exercise and walk in accordance with faith which is the confident conviction and assurance in the power, ability, and willingness of God to manifest all things including that which appears impossible.

The mantle is not just for you. It is not only to cover and protect you from the influence of the world around you, but also evidence to those who encounter you. Others will see and acknowledge the difference about you. They will see what God is doing in you and through you.

Here is another important lesson to note from the biblical text. The text alludes to the existence of Elijah's other children in ministry, other prophets who studied under Elijah, but the mantle was only given to Elisha. What has been assigned to you is for you. The only person who has the authority to take it from you is you if you choose to not pick it up and wear it, or if you cast it away through reckless abandon.

The mantle of this calling is not for everyone. I wondered why none of the other prophets of Elijah were considered to receive his holy garment. The Spirit reminded me that not everyone can manage the weight, the responsibility or accountability, of ministry to the masses. God has appointed you and anointed you for this task and at this time to wear the garment, not with arrogant pride but with humility and humbleness of your spirit.

{ 5 }

The Power of "Let"

Ephesians 4:29-32 (RSV)

[29] Let no evil talk come out of your mouths, but only such as is good for edifying, as fits the occasion, that it may impart grace to those who hear. [30] And do not grieve the Holy Spirit of God, in whom you were sealed for the day of redemption. [31] Let all bitterness and wrath and anger and clamor and slander be put away from you, with all malice, [32] and be kind to one another, tenderhearted, forgiving one another, as God in Christ forgave you.

You do not have the authority nor the ability to give God permission. Eradicate that notion from your mind. God is sovereign. We cannot manipulate infinite wisdom and authority with our finite perspectives, attitudes, desires, and presumptions. The will of God is supreme and supersedes all that you desire. God does not seek permission from creation to do anything. Despite our technological advancements all of creation remains subject to God. As the sovereign authority and presence throughout the universe, God needs nothing from us but our compliance and willingness to fulfill God's plan.

As children, we often extended cordial invitation to others to join or accompany us in various activities using statements such as, "Let us go" or "Let us do." Such statements incite feelings of warmth, acceptance, and inclusion. Within each statement, there is the implication for an action or activity to commence together, not in isolation, not apart from, but together, united, in concert with one another.

Moreover, each statement began with the word "let" as an invitational welcome or bidding to another to participate or collaborate in an activity. In fact, this use of "let" is found throughout the biblical text in statements of welcome and invitation into a shared activity. Consider the following biblical texts:

Psalm 122:1 (NIV)
> [1] I was glad when they said unto me, "Let us go into the house of the Lord."

Isaiah 1:18 (KJV)
> [18] "Come now, and let us reason together," saith the Lord: "though your sins be as scarlet, they shall be as white as snow; though they be red like crimson, they shall be as wool."

In both verses, an invitation was thereby extended through an implicit message resulting in the doing of an explicit action. Let demands action response. As God speaks to us, and through us, the word of God in our lives demands active response and engagement.

As we seek to explore and understand the calling and responsibility of those called to the office of a prophet and those anointed to do prophetic works through the power of God, we must understand the power of let as an invitation to mobilize and respond. This is not a power nor authority that belongs to you. The power of let is an authority to which you must submit and thereby live.

Notice the action of the word let. The Merriam-Webster Diction defines the word "let" to mean, "To cause to; to give opportunity to or fail to prevent; to free from or as if from confinement; to permit to enter, pass, or leave; to make an adjustment to." It is outward in its focus and direction. It flows from in an outward direction from a source of production and produces and evidentiary actions and substantive proof. Let is not stagnant; it is vibrant and vivacious, full of prognosticating potential and perpetuated power. It is efficacious in its zeal to do, act, respond, produce, and provide. Although "let" is a small word, it possesses a deeply embedded power and authority to shift, change, and create.

Let is nothing new; it is how we have become. When we read the first chapter of the Book of Genesis, the story of beginnings, we must take heed of the power of let in the text. According to the Hebrew word found in the Genesis text, hâyâh, there exists great authority and potential in the word. Our cognitive understanding of this word is most impactful when we take a moment to fully digest what the author of the biblical text was saying about the power of let – the power of the spoken word of God.

According to the Strong's Hebrew Lexicon, hâyâh (pronounced haw-yaw) means "to be, become, come to pass, exist, happen, fall out; to come into being." Anticipated action, or divine resolve, follows every "let" spoken by God. Hear what the writer of the Genesis account recorded concerning the power of let:

Genesis 1:3-26 (RSV)
> And God said,
> Let there be light.
> Let there be a dome amid the waters, and let it separate the waters from the waters.
> Let the waters under the sky be gathered into one place, and let the dry land appear.
> Let the earth put forth vegetation: plants yielding seed, and fruit trees of every kind on earth that bear fruit with the seed in it.
> Let there be lights in the dome of the sky to separate the day from the night; and let them be for signs and for seasons and

for days and years and let them be lights in the dome of the
sky to give light upon the earth.

Let the waters bring forth swarms of living creatures, and let
birds fly above the earth across the dome of the sky.

Let birds multiply on the earth.

Let the earth bring forth living creatures of every kind.

Let us make humankind in our image, according to our likeness;
and let them have dominion over the fish of the sea, and
over the birds of the air, and over the cattle, and over all the
wild animals of the earth, and over every creeping thing that
creeps upon the earth.

There is a cadence in this text, a melody to the supernatural greatness and authority of God. It is a message of action and timeless
movement towards something greater and better. Let is powerful when
spoken in true divine authority.

The message of Genesis is not one of probable or potential authority; God's word is our sovereign, proven, perfected, and purposeful
authority. Therefore, in reading and understanding the message of
God and the biblical text, it is imperative to note that the word of
God moves with intentionality and yields purposeful outcomes for the
believer. Every let spoken by God yielded a manifested action establishing order and the rules of productivity. With each statement from
God as the Creative Authority of all that is, promissory power resides.
Yes, and it is so.

When God speaks, it is so.

The "let" of God initiates activity in the physical realm. When
God speaks, the universe responds. What we are witnessing in Genesis
Chapter 1 is the transcendental authority of the word of God, not the
Bible as we read it in its diluted and transliterated state, but the supe-
riority of the words spoken by God which have resounded throughout
time and space throughout all eternity.

One may ask, "How powerful are the words of God?" Imagine the most intellectual engaged in thinking. The words which proceed from the mouth of God originated within the mind of God which is the epitome of omniscience. For the Holy and Omniscient One to formulate words, which, for the person of God, existed merely as thoughts contrived in the mind of God which manifested into being, demonstrates the magnitude and complexity of God's divinity and authority. The Book of Genesis is a human attempt to articulate and to explain that which transpired within the mind of God. That which manifests before us reflects the very heart of God.

Words have profound power. Even the very words that you speak have power. As the mouthpiece of God in the office of a prophet, the words that you speak possess God-given authority. This is proof that there is power in your words. For this reason, you must ever so careful and mindful of the words that you speak over, and into, the lives of others, even yourself. Choose your words wisely and speak under the unction of God and only as God has ordained you to do. Your words have power, but misspoken words also have consequences.

The prophet cannot abuse the authority or sheer power of the words which they allow to come forth. There is an expedient authority sealed in the mouth of the prophet. The words of the prophet, spoken in the Name of the Lord, have the divine authority and potential to be and to become. Your words are glazed with the divine wisdom of God and infused with supernatural authority not of your own.

Genesis speaks of the spoken word of God but does not capture the complexity or dynamics of what transpired. For one thing, it is not meant to know or understand everything about the movement of God. Our faith must bear us up and transport us where our rational capabilities lack ability to reason and resolve. Through the difficult moments and hard to understand conflicts of our lives, God remains faithful and true. The psalmist said it this way,

Psalm 46:1-3 (NIV)

¹ God is our refuge and strength,
  an ever-present help in trouble.
² Therefore we will not fear, though the earth give way
  and the mountains fall into the heart of the sea,
³ though its waters roar and foam
  and the mountains quake with their surging.

We remain steadfast and confident in the power of God. It is God who alone possesses the power to speak words that will heal, deliver, release, transform, build, establish, maintain, sustain, redeem, restore, renew, and revive the hope that rests within us. We cannot give up nor give in. That is the message of the psalmist, do not ever give up.

In the womb of your mother, in the moment of conception, the power of let began working in you to create and assign greatness within you. Before you were formed in your mother's womb, God already knew you. The Lord ordained you for such a time, purpose, and calling. This is not a vocation. The prophet's call is a divine appointment. You are here and have made it through because God chose you.

Even through your struggles, tragedies, adversities, obstacles, hardships, heartaches, disappointments, calamities, set-backs, hurts, fears, mistakes, and everything else that you have experienced, God spoke the word of your deliverance. God spoke the words into the atmosphere of your being and into the DNA of your circumstances. A divine unction and promise succeeded every "let." Each has manifested into who you are in this hour and moment.

Beloved, you are not what you have been through. You are the living word of God. You exemplify the power of let, as God has spoken over your life. It does not remove the complexity or difficulty of our circumstances, nor the adversarial presence lurking around all that we endeavor, nor the pain, guilt, shame, or remorse we harbor within us. The power of let is that it provides us hope and potential for better days ahead. The earth was without form and void...it was the habitation of nothingness and darkness. However, let was spoken and released into the atmosphere of the universe, thus breaking, and delivering the earth from the despair of its former void state. The power of God manifested and all that we know came into being.

If you and I are ever to become or come into divine being as the prophetic authorities which we have been called, anointed, and appointed to be, we must the power of let reign supreme within and through us knowing that God is at work within us. Your whole self which means all that makes you who you are including your thoughts, actions, ways, beliefs, fears, and desires must be surrendered to the power and authority of God.

You are not your own. Your hopes and dreams must rest in God as the sole source of your survival. Beloved, the power of the word let, when spoken from the mouth of God, alters the very state of our being and very existence. It transforms the fabric of lives by mending the tattered pieces of our experiences into a blanket of endless possibilities.

God extended grace over your life. It was released into your spirit and over your life as God declared "let" to the atmosphere of your soul's hope. The emancipation of your soul from the destructive clutches of sinful desire and pleasures was granted when God said "let."

Let broke and demolished the chains which constrained you and the walls which have confined you preventing you from growing and becoming what God has divinely and uniquely purposed for your life. Let has been on your side, moving things away from you, changing things around you, shifting seasons for you, aligning promises for you, even when you did not deserve it, let never abandoned or aborted you. Let continues to live within you and through you and it keeps fighting for you, making ways for you, overcoming obstacles, and defeating enemies on your behalf.

John 14:1 (NKJV)

¹ "Let not your heart be troubled; you believe in God, believe also in Me."

Acts 28:28 (NKJV)

28 Let it, therefore, be known to you that the salvation of God has been sent to the Gentiles, and they will hear it!

Romans 3:4 (NKJV)

4 Let God be true but every man a liar.

Romans 12:6-7,9 (NKJV)

6 Having then gifts differing according to the grace that is given to us, let us use them: if prophecy, let us prophesy in proportion to our faith;

7 or ministry, let us use it in our ministering; he who teaches, in teaching...

9 Let love be without hypocrisy. Abhor what is evil. Cling to what is good.

Philippians 2:3,5 (NKJV)

3 Let nothing be done through selfish ambition or conceit, but in lowliness of mind let each esteem others better than himself...

5 Let this mind be in you which was also in Christ Jesus.

Beloved, you must consider within yourself if and how committed you are to the calling now placed upon your life. God's calling is sure. It requires surety in your response and engagement to the office you aspire to hold. There is no time for wavering faith or questionable accountability and allegiance to the same. It comes with great sacrifice of more than just your time and resources, but the cost of your soul's peace, your sanity, your space, your social ties, all that comprises who you are and hope to be, as well as an undeniable weight of responsibility. You are not your own, and all that you have no longer belongs to you. God's prophetic calling requires all of you.

Let God have God's way in and through you. Let God have total control of you. Let God be the answer that brings fulfillment to deep caverns of your soul, satisfying your longings as well as your hopes and quelching your fears and apprehensions.

The word "Let" proceeds from the mouth of God and moves at the unction and under the authority of God, Creator of the Universe. Let God abide in you. Let God reign in you. Let God shine and speak through you. Beloved, let the power of God overtake you and shift you into your greatest becoming. However, to become your best self, it will not be easy, and it will require your vulnerability, but you must allow the power of let to accomplish its perfect work in your life. Let go of your pain, your past, your hurts, your fears, your failures, your mistakes, your discomforts...let go!

Surrender.

I Hear the Lord Calling

Romans 8:26-30 (NIV)

²⁶ In the same way, the Spirit helps us in our weakness. We do not know what we ought to pray for, but the Spirit himself intercedes for us through wordless groans. ²⁷ And he who searches our hearts knows the mind of the Spirit, because the Spirit intercedes for God's people in accordance with the will of God. ²⁸ And we know that in all things God works for the good of those who love him, who have been called according to his purpose. ²⁹ For those God foreknew he also predestined to be conformed to the image of his Son, that he might be the firstborn among many brothers and sisters. ³⁰ And those he predestined, he also called; those he called, he also justified; those he justified, he also glorified.

If public recognition and notoriety or material gain are the impetus behind your drive and motivation for the office of the prophet, stop where you are. The prophetic mantle requires self-sacrifice and the surrender of your total self to the will and plan of God. You cannot be self-appointed to this work, nor can you rely on the benefits of social promotion and popularity among people. True prophets must hear and answer the calling from God through divine unction.

Ephesians 4:11-13 (NIV)

[11] So Christ himself gave the apostles, the prophets, the evangelists, the pastors, and teachers,

[12] to equip his people for works of service, so that the body of Christ may be built up,

[13] until we all reach unity in the faith and in the knowledge of the Son of God and become mature, attaining to the whole measure of the fullness of Christ.

The Lord calls and appoints, chooses, and anoints those who shall serve in this selfless office. The prophet hears, sees, knows, and must convey God's messages to the people. You are the mandated reporter of the oracles and wisdom of God; you are the human voice of spiritual authority and divine greatness. As prophet you are the living shofar sounding the alarm of heaven through obedience to wisdom of God swelling within your belly, words seeking release to transform the hearts and minds of the people of God.

Prophetic calling embodies and magnifies the will of God in the world; it does not respond in accordance with your pride, arrogance, self-centeredness, self-absorption, or any such characteristic. This is not the work of the selfish or foolish. The calling of a prophet is the awakening of the soul. It is the revival of the spirit. It the harvesting of spiritual giftings and potential. It is the evolution of the self on the internal quest for a defined purpose. It is the sounding forth of deliverance and hope in a present age. It is the denunciation of a self-agenda and surrender to God's divine agenda and plan for your life.

Not everyone can bear or uphold the weight of this calling. Sounding prophetic and operating under the authority the divine calling and unction to serve as a prophet do not mean the same thing. They are not synonymous. As individuals rooted in the steep traditions, rituals, and doctrines of mainstream denominationalism, we must strive to avoid seeking titles and positions for the mere sake of having one. Titles do not make us important, nor do titles validate your existence. It is the quality and integrity of the work that we do which qualify us for the titles that we endeavor to carry. There is no expectation for prophets to be favorites, preferred, liked, or even desired. The words of true prophets may often cut harshly or sound insensitive, but their words deliver correction and establish divine order within the household of faith.

We can no more assume someone a prophet simply because they sound prophetic or because they make prophetic statements than we can determine someone has an apostolic mantle because they assist in establishing ministries. These are assumptions, and I will even dare say mistakes, that we make in church/religious culture. You are not an apostle simply because you help cultivate ideas. It is impossible to be truly apostolic when you lack the ability to commit and dedicate the whole of yourself (time, talents, and treasures) to the building and establishment of ministry even though your name may not be displayed on the marquee. Apostles did more than spew ideas. They were first-hand in the process and the sacrifice of establishing and maintaining ministries. However, I will save that discussion for another book.

This work is about the prophet's call. Anyone can sound prophetic. Sounding prophetic and wearing vestments and colors does not make one a prophet. The prophet's call demands drastic life changes, soul surrender, and mind liberation to be fully accessible to hear the voice of the Lord. It requires the individual acknowledging the call to live through periods of isolation, often ostracized from and by others simply because you (we) are clearly, unquestionably, undeniably, and unmistakably peculiar people.

We just do not fit in. We can be in a room full of people and still feel alone. My loneliest moments in life have been while surrounded by people who did not share or value the anointing of God upon my life; I was present yet alone in a room full of people. Sometimes we force ourselves to interact with others simply to feel part of a larger group. However, we lack genuine interest in the things discussed or found entertaining by those around us. Because we have been separated and sanctified for the work of God, we are peculiar which prevents our ability to fully engage in general social activity.

Nevertheless, while interacting with others, our minds are often on a distant quest for the Spirit of God, for the clarity of direction, or for understanding of the whispering voice of God that we hear in every room. Our bodies are often present, but our minds and spirits have detached from the present physical surroundings and activities. The mind and spirit continually pursue a spiritual quest for Kingdom assignments and understanding of the movement of God throughout the land. Those who possess the prophetic mantle find strength and acceptance when we are engaged in the activities which feed and minister to our souls, not our flesh.

Prophets cannot spiritually, nor physically, escape God's presence. In your efforts to flee the commission and mandate of God, you may make futile efforts to hide from God, but we are never out of the eyesight of God, nor are we so hidden that God cannot and will not hear us when we cry out to God. God remains ever near and a very present help in our times of trouble, doubt, depression, and dismay. There is a Psalm which comes to mind when I think about the inescapable presence of God. In this Psalm, the prophet, after critical self-examination and careful analysis of his present predicament and vast situations in which he had placed himself in efforts to avoid and flee the presence of God, declared,

Psalm 139 (NIV)

[1] You have searched me, Lord,
    and you know me.
[2] You know when I sit and when I rise;
    you perceive my thoughts from afar.

³ You discern my going out and my lying down;
    you are familiar with all my ways.
⁴ Before a word is on my tongue
    you, Lord, know it completely.
⁵ You hem me in behind and before,
    and you lay your hand upon me.
⁶ Such knowledge is too wonderful for me,
    too lofty for me to attain.
⁷ Where can I go from your Spirit?
    Where can I flee from your presence?
⁸ If I go up to the heavens, you are there;
    if I make my bed in the depths, you are there.

Although God remains omniscient for all, this knowledge bears a heavier burden and weight upon the prophet. Prophets struggle to fit in and to assimilate trying to be like others and to enjoy the pleasures of life others appear to enjoy. Like David, prophets go through life continuously petitioning God for the answer to the question, "Where can I go from your Spirit?"

David, by far, was not an innocent individual. He was king and prophet, constantly in battle between two opposing dichotomies. David wore the robe of an earthly king which afforded him prestige, power, and position as well as entitled him to certain pleasures and privileges, yet at his core he bore the divine appointment and assignment as a prophet. Even when he submitted to his flesh to pursue royal pleasures and to fulfill his duties as a king, war raged within his very being.

If you have an opportunity to read and comprehend the life of David, you will discover that David battled within himself constantly. Remember, in the natural, David was not only a king but a son, brother, husband, father, and a prophet. God called and appointed. Scholars attributed a great substantial amount of The Psalms to the authorship of King David. Through the Psalms, David dealt with his internal struggles and conflicts as both king and prophet, as a natural man and as a man with a divine calling and appointment on his life.

The dichotomy and complexity of David's struggle reveals the ongoing battles and struggles we all experience between our flesh and the anointing on our lives. He wrestled within over his decisions and actions. He contemplated. The conflict was between his human desires and pleasures and the prophet that God called to be. David battled tirelessly to resolve these conflicts. His duties and accountability as a king along with the weight and pull of his spiritual assignment influenced and impacted him on multiple levels; however, it did not sever his relationship with or his trust in the Lord.

Because of the uniqueness of this assignment, not everyone possesses the ability or fortitude needed to fulfill the challenges set forth. I remember as a young struggling seminarian, one of my professors, Dr. Michael D, assigned a reading assignment to our Field Internship class, one which permanently changed my understanding of my spiritual assignment. We were tasked to read, discuss, and reflect upon the book by Dr. Henri Nouwen, "Can You Drink the Cup." In fact, the book was so insightful that I have recommended it to others, particularly those I have had privilege to mentor in ministry. Although the book is small in length, its message is major. This book remains one of the most impactful books I have ever read as relates to my personal acknowledgement, understanding, and acceptance of the responsibility and level of accountability placed upon my life in ministry.

Beloved, your assignment from God must have priority over the very battles and struggles you face in your personal life. Every person who struggles with this divine calling must determine for him/herself the time of readiness to accept the weight of the call. The assignment as a prophet must outweigh the satisfaction and gratification you receive from being socially accessible and accepted. When it comes down to it, the soul of the prophet would rather be earthly relevant through spiritual accountability rather than socially acceptable and awarded for popularity. Do not confuse or mistake your attachments for your assignment. The assignment is greater and will release greatness in your life and the lives of those to whom you minister and prophesy.

Throughout this book, I will reference the stories of different biblical prophets to provide sound understanding of the life and calling of prophets from a biblical standpoint. The biblical story of Samuel is notably one of the best and most admired narratives capturing the irony and uniqueness of the prophetic calling.

In Chapter 3 of the First Book of Samuel, the story of his calling can be found. The calling of Samuel has always fascinated me. I can relate to and understand Samuel's experience as depicted in the text. Samuel's story is personal to me; it mirrors my own experience and calling from God. In fact, if we would take time to become truly intimate with the biblical text, each of us will find ourselves in the pages of the text. There is a character within the biblical story who captures and characterizes our lives, one whose story is our story.

The story of Samuel and his calling experience was one of the first Bible stories in which I was able to see myself. As a young Black boy, born to a single parent, raised with generational influences of strong Black women, in a poor, drug-infested, crime-ridden, neighborhood known as "The Hole in the Wall," envisioning myself in the biblical text was not always easy. More importantly, I did see myself as gifted to be one of God's chosen few.

Nevertheless, it was through the story of Samuel that I later resolved that what I had been hearing was God. I heard God speaking. I heard God calling my name. I was not going crazy hearing my name called by a voice unseen from within the darkness of my bedroom and even in the whispering of the winds which blew around me as I walked within nature or rested along the babbling of wooded streams. From Samuel's story, I found consolation and assurance knowing that God was speaking to me, calling me, beckoning to me, acknowledging my frail and broken existence. To me, a small dark-skinned Black boy with eyeglasses from a broken, dysfunctional, and economically challenged home, God was speaking, and God was insistently calling.

Who would have ever thought that the same boy that people, including those in his very bloodline, had overlooked and had disregarded, God would see and choose to use? Disregarded because of the rich dark tone of his skin, wide forehead, full lips, and the circumstances of his existence, yet the one through whom God would choose to operate and establish God's Kingdom. Who would have ever thought this would be possible?

I am a witness that God chooses the least likely among us to dumbfound and impact the world. I have a greater appreciation of the promise or purpose and destiny delivered by the Apostle Paul which states,

1 Corinthians 2:9 (NKJV)

But as it is written: "Eye has not seen, nor ear heard, nor have entered into the heart of man the things which God has prepared for those who love Him."

If I could receive the prophet's call, you can too. God sees in us what others may choose to ignore about us. The potential and promise of your purpose pose a threat to the insecurities of your enemies, haters, and perpetrators. That is not your problem. God does not focus on what or who you are in the present. God sees, knows, and seeks to develop who you shall be and who you shall become. Regardless of how others see us or receive us, God perfects the imperfections of our character, our status, our experiences, our flaws and mistakes, and the state of our natural beings.

Through the all-surpassing power of the Holy Spirit, God infuses the abundance of grace and unexplainable favor and embeds us into God's plan of righteous forgiveness, redemption, deliverance, life, love, hope, and salvation. You may not have been much to others, and you still may not be. In fact, there are those who will never acknowledge the potential of your calling, but God sees the value in you. Ministry will demand that you operate under the pain and agony of your own scars, scars caused by your failed trust in others and of yourself. Nevertheless, God sees the worth of your scars.

Samuel was a product of the church who began operating in ministry in the church at an early age during a season when the voice of the Lord had become silent and uncommon. According to the story, Samuel fell asleep in the house of the Lord. He was aroused from his sleep by a voice subtly calling his name. He assumed the voice calling to him through the night was that of his teacher and pastor, Eli. As a resolute and eager young assistant in the House of the Lord, Samuel arose suddenly from his sleep and responded to the voice calling unto him by running quickly to Eli, "Here I am, you called me." Eli assured him, that it was not him who was calling Samuel. This happened to him throughout the night. It was not until Eli stepped out of his own flesh to understand what was transpiring in the life of Samuel. It was then that Eli provided Samuel with the guidance he needed to respond to God's calling. Eli instructed him, "Go and lie down, and if he calls you, say, 'Speak, Lord, for your servant is listening.'"

Have you responded to the whisper of God summoning and beckoning to you, calling you from your bed of complacence? Do you hear, more importantly, are you listening to what the Lord is saying to you in this season and in this hour? The winds of time are shifting and changing, and God continues calling to you seeking to elevate you, and to catapult your thinking, so you can become the greatness of God's glory. Are you listening?

Do you find yourself relying on, or waiting on, the wisdom and validation of others before you make the decision to listen and respond to the voice of the Lord for yourself? Be honest with yourself for a moment. Have you, like so many of us, wasted valuable time and resources as well as your talents and anointing as you chase tirelessly after emptiness? Do not allow your living to be in vain. God has called you for greater. You have lost time reaching running with and futilely responding to those who see you but fail to truly know or understand who or what you are? They do not and cannot comprehend God's anointing on your life.

I need to share with you a lesson from the story of Samuel. Samuel operated in ministry under the leadership and authority of a pastor, a teacher, and a guide. The season of renegade prophets and ministers has ended. Training, development, and accountability are critical factors in the life of minsters and especially prophets. In the current dispensation of the move of God, there will be a return to order and structure. Leaders are accountable to those they lead and those who seek offices of leadership in the household of faith must adhere to structure, substance, and stability as vessels of God's using.

Furthermore, Samuel's life in ministry and in his development as a prophet reveals something completely different and revolutionary about ministry, and those at work in the church in ministry. There are people working within the church, who do not yet know the Lord, and those who operate in ministry based solely on individual talents, gifts, or desires, but not with the anointing or authorization of the Spirit of the Lord. According to the story of Samuel, in the first verse he is clearly identified as one who "ministered before the Lord," yet, verses later his relationship with God is addressed, "Now Samuel did not yet know the Lord: The word of the Lord had not yet been revealed to him."

Our paths to the discovery of who God is comes at distinctly various times in our lives. There are those who were taught to have a relationship with God early in life, while others come to know God through their circumstances and situations. Strong relationships are often forged out of our experiences and the overcoming of our circumstances. This is much like the parable spoken by Jesus about the workers in the vineyard who received invitations at various times throughout the day, but all received equal wages. It matters not when or how we came into relationship with the Lord to do the work of the Lord, the important thing is that we come to have a personal relationship with God. The truth is, there are people who by reason of their upbringing were raised in the church to have a personal relationship with God, yet their character, actions, attitude, and behavior fail to exemplify the relationship they profess.

Samuel did not know the Lord when he began his ministry in the house of God. In other words, Samuel was working for God but had no established relationship with the Lord. He had heard about YHWH but lacked understanding thereof. So many of us embarked upon this journey of ministry, serving in one capacity or another in the church, yet we had no conceptual or relational understanding of God. Who is God? We knew of God based on what they told and taught us while attending weekly worship services, Sunday School, Bible class, youth meetings, and from hearing generations before us pray and testify. However, our personal relationship with God in the fullness of who God is manifests and evolves over time through our experiences and our personal relationship with God. As our lives and our purpose materialize and take shape, God in us becomes more real and visible.

Even in the absence of relationship with God, God had chosen you and implanted within you an anointing for this season. The circumstances of our lives will often bring us to the place of revelation. Samuel's life had been promised to the service of God as an offering from his mother Hannah to God. Hannah made an oath before she conceived Samuel within her womb. I share that with you because while you are doubting and disbelieving the calling on your life and whispering voice you hear bidding you to "Come forth!" God is answering the prayers of those who came before you, those who prayed to God for you and for your arrival. Your life was an offering to God before your mother's conceived you in her womb. And now is the season in which the manifestation of answered prayers is being fulfilled in and through you.

Take note, however, before Samuel was able receive the prophetic mantle and divine assignment, he had to first come to know God for himself. Beloved, it is not enough to rely on the knowledge and relationship of others with God. For God to use you and to elevate you to your rightful the place of divine appointment, you must experience the transforming power of divine encounter with God. To speak for God, you must know God personally. Spiritual transformation must take place in your life, your life goals, as well as your perspectives in life. Whoever you sought to be and all that you sought to become in life must change so you may become the spiritual agent that God has called you to be in this season.

According to the story of Samuel, the first few times that he heard the voice calling to him, Samuel responded to Eli. Samuel directed his responsive intentions and efforts to the wrong individual. Like Samuel, people are guilty of this very infraction, misdirected faith. We hear God, but responded to individuals for their acknowledgement, acceptance, and affirmation when we need to respond to God.

Too many of us have been operating in the church, engaging in full time ministry, and yet we lack the conviction of true relationship of the Lord. Servants of God functioning the house of the Lord not knowing the voice of God sounds like an oxymoron. However, I suggest that it was a set up for greater. Such actions aid in the unfolding of God's divine plan for your surrender, salvation, and redemption. The Holy Spirit must verify and qualify your calling and your conviction to the work of the temple.

It takes one who has experienced true transformation to preach transformation in the lives of others. Consequently, the transformative power of the Holy Spirit will come upon us to shift our thinking and perceptions of ourselves and what God can accomplish in and through us. A divine encounter remains a dire need in the church. If there is a desire to lead within the body of believers, the need to for personal transformation remains paramount. Ministry on every level focuses on God and the fulfillment of God's purpose. We must avoid the temptation to become consumed with satisfying and pleasing people more than pleasing and honoring God.

Beloved, your actions of disobedience have delayed, not denied, the development of the spiritual ambassador lying dormant within you.

As one who started in ministry incredibly early in life, I can speak to you from personal experience. My mother shared the story with me of how one of my uncles held me as an infant and declared that there was an anointing on me to preach the Gospel and to serve God as a musician.

I spent years trying to please and satisfy the expectations of others on my life. I knew God, but the transformative encounter with God came later in life as I found myself stripped naked and ashamed before God and then I was able to hear the voice of God concerning my assignment clearly for myself. God demands your deliverance from the approval of other people. You must castrate your selfish desires and ambitious ego from the very fabric of your heart so you can fully avail yourself for God's service.

There are times when God must put us in places in which the spiritual distractions around us become nonexistent so the Spirit of God can illuminate within us. All of what you have experienced, all that you lost, the relationship that nearly destroyed you, the broken promises which shattered your emotional well-being, the diagnosis that could have killed you, the encounters which could have potentially taken everything you have worked for; all these things have been creating and establishing within you an exceeding weight of glory for the greater work of God's Kingdom. As a prophet, what you have endured and overcome strengthens your witness and extends credibility to your prophetic voice. In fact, the Apostle Paul had this to say about overcoming obstacles and setbacks,

2 Corinthians 4:16-18 (NIV)

Therefore, we do not lose heart. Though outwardly we are wasting away, yet inwardly we are being renewed day by day. For our light and momentary troubles are achieving for us an eternal glory that far outweighs them all. So, we fix our eyes not on what is seen, but on what is unseen, since what is seen is temporary, but what is unseen is eternal.

Beloved, everything you have been through, all that life has handed you has been worth it. There is value in your pain and your struggle, but more importantly, there is hope through your overcoming.

Money, social influence, and popularity have no bearing in spiritual matters. The obtaining of certain abilities and blessings can only come through the Spirit. It takes the sound spiritual authority of God to grow and develop the spiritual vessel within these clay houses of ours. Become acquainted with the power of God serves as preventative maintenance against suffering the dangers of misguidance.

To be God's prophet, you must know God. You must fasten your allegiance, devotion, and commitment on pleasing and satisfying God, not people. The prophets of God must have familiarity with and clear understanding and knowledge of the voice of the Lord. Sheep produce sheep. However, sheep know the sound of their shepherd's voice and are able and willing to follow the shepherd's leading and guiding.

To every undercover prophet, those who wrestle with the calling of God on your lives because out of fear, God is calling. Like Samuel, the calling of God does not subside. God is persistent. God's persistence demonstrates God's continuous love, trust, and faith in you to operate and to thrive as God's anointed vessel.

God does not call us because we are perfect, favored, liked, talented, or good. The Lord calls and qualifies those whom God has deemed worthy whose integrity outweigh their egos. God personally anoints those whom God knows can holster the weight of God's glory and remain humble and touchable servants in the life of the Kingdom. People may never choose to recognize you, or your potential, and they may try to deny you the privilege of serving in the temple for their own self-righteous reasons. One thing I have discovered about human nature is that people find it easier to judge and condemn others rather than face the truth of their own failures and inadequacies. God, however, is not like people.

The same God who remains rich in everlasting mercy and continuously extends unmerited grace and favor upon you has summoned you to serve humbly or wholeheartedly. To those God has called, God has promised to equip you with all you will need for the work ahead.

1 Peter 5:6-10 (ESV)

> Humble yourselves, therefore, under the mighty hand of God so that at the proper time God may exalt you, casting all your anxieties on the Lord, because the Lord cares for you. Be sober minded; be watchful. Your adversary the devil prowls around like a roaring lion, seeking someone to devour. Resist him, firm in your faith, knowing that the same kinds of suffering are being experienced by your [fellow believers] throughout the world. And after you have suffered a little while, the God of all grace, who has called you to God's eternal glory in Christ, will restore, confirm, strengthen, and establish you.

Who you are, and whom God has called and ordained you in the Spirit to be, suffers no limitations because of your mistakes, flaws, humanity, indecisions, or imperfections! Beloved, do you hear the Lord calling?

Despite what you have been through, the mistakes you have made along the way, or the perceptions of others toward you, God is calling you and has appointed you in this hour. Do you hear the prophet's call upon your life, the unction to speak the mysteries of God to unveil the truth of God within a god-filled world? As God is calling you, there are souls awaiting you.

{ 7 }

Making the Sacrifice

Hebrews 13:11-16 (NIV)

¹¹ The high priest carries the blood of animals into the Most Holy Place as a sin offering, but the bodies are burned outside the camp. ¹² And so Jesus also suffered outside the city gate to make the people holy through his own blood. ¹³ Let us, then, go to him outside the camp, bearing the disgrace he bore. ¹⁴ For here we do not have an enduring city, but we are looking for the city that is to come. ¹⁵ Through Jesus, therefore, let us continually offer to God a sacrifice of praise—the fruit of lips that openly profess his name. ¹⁶ And do not forget to do good and to share with others, for with such sacrifices God is pleased.

People will attempt to walk in the office of a prophet but will fall short of the calling and abandon the mantle. Research has proven that in recent years, more faith leaders have walked away from their pulpits and positions within the Kingdom. More churches are closing each year than churches are opening. Not only have ministries closed and ministers have quit the ministry, but suicidal ideation has become more prevalent in the church and particularly among faith leaders. The unfortunate truth is that not everyone is equipped to manage the demands of prophetic leadership and ministry, nor are they ready to make the total sacrifice.

There is a price and a cost which must be honored and satisfied. To receive from God, you must surrender and sacrifice yourself to God. Ministry requires great sacrifices. Jesus explained in a parable found in Luke 14 that before you engage in the work, it behooves you to count the cost. You must have full understanding of what you are embarking upon and the demands that will be placed upon your life. Not that you will comprehend or have intimate knowledge of the distinctive aspects of your calling, but you must seek understanding of the expectations placed upon you. This is a work like no other. It bears a weight uncommon to others. It demands personal sacrifices for the sake of the soul salvation of others.

Do you think you can truly manage what God demands of you? Do you have the inherent stamina and spiritual fortitude needed to bear the weight and price of this ministry? Like Abraham, who was willing to sacrifice his own son on a mountainside in obedience to God's calling upon his life, each of us must obey the calling of God at whatever cost making the sacrifice demanded for blessings and bounty of the prophetic calling upon our lives. This is not a group or collective duty; this is an individualize moment of spiritual accountability and duty of personal service to God and to the assignment God has given you.

Beloved, enter ministry well-advised fully comprehending the nature of the prophetic call; the work is divine. The status of your soul will shift, and the blood placed upon your life will increase. If your goal and ambition are to make a profit, either you have not been called to be a prophet, or you have misappropriated your gift and anointing. For such, there are dire spiritual consequences, the costs of your spiritual denial and abandonment. This is a calling, a spiritual appointment, not an endeavor, gig, task, venture, job, or hobby. At the heart of such ministry rests the undeniable demand for sacrifice; you are your own greatest sacrifice. The life of the true prophet is selfless; God commands the heart and the prophet.

Perfection is not God's expectation. God knows you are a flawed vessel, marred, and even fragmented in areas of your life. However, the experience of the Prophet Jeremiah in the home of the potter shapes the faith and spirit of the broken prophet. Even in your brokenness, you still have immense value, worth, and potential. Therefore, we must embrace and embark upon the prophetic appointment humbly and reverently. Your service as a prophet of God demands the sacrifice of yourself.

For those who hear the prophet's call, the words of Apostle Paul resound differently and should reach the apex of your spiritual self-awareness.

Romans 12:1-2 (CEV)

Dear friends, God is good. So, I beg you to offer your bodies to God as a living sacrifice, pure and pleasing. That is the most sensible way to serve God. Do not be like the people of this world, but let God change the way you think. Then you will know how to do everything that is good and pleasing to God.

Ministry in every form requires humble submission. However, the success of the prophet to fulfill the divine mandate placed upon his or her life will vary. Success may not manifest as one would think or desire. Each person called to prophesy must manage and maintain leverage and define spiritual balance in their lives. No one can do it for you; you must remember yourself in the process to avoid the catastrophe of spiritual and emotional burnout. You are prophet, a human agent of divine purpose, not a superhuman with supernatural powers. Balance and intentionality are critical. Yes, you must die to yourself, your own agenda, desires, and ego, but God does not intend for you to die in the process for failing to effectively balance the duties and responsibilities of life and ministry.

In the coming pages, I am going to share with you the definition and distinctions among prophets. But consider this, if you will, prophets must resign self. Nothing about you remains your own. This is not to provide a negative depiction prophetic ministry, nor is this to discourage you in any way from accepting your calling. God has purposed me to reveal and share truths surrounding the prophetic call. No one enlightened me with such wisdom when I said yes to the call. I learned along the way, striking walls, losing momentum, disappointing people, but remaining submitted to God for redirection and restoration as deemed necessary.

Beloved, we are blessed. The Holy Spirit reveals all things and brings all things to the forefront of our minds. Therefore, the aim of my sharing is to dispel myths of promising grandeur and material prosperity associated with the prophetic office amidst this sea of prosperity preachers. Yes, prophets prophesy about the coming of prosperity, we prophesy like Elijah about the coming of rain in dry seasons, but material gain is not what we do, and certainly not what we proclaim.

Matthew 6:19-21 (CEV)

Do not store up treasures on earth! Moths and rust can destroy them, and thieves can break in and steal them. Instead, store up your treasures in heaven, where moths and rust cannot destroy them, and thieves cannot break in and steal them. Your heart will always be where your treasure is.

Mark 8:36-37, (NIV)

What good is it for someone to gain the entire world, yet forfeit their soul? Or what can anyone give in exchange for their soul?

Prophets must remain relevant. The rhema word that flows forth from the mouth of the prophet must originate in the heart of the prophet through the inspiration of the Spirit of God. Rather than material wealth, God's prophet must effectively articulate the heart of God. God has ordained prophets to encourage and to deliver prosperity to the human soul. It is within the confines of the soul in which the flames of hope and determination ignite causing an inferno of zealous possibilities. When we revive the soul, the body (the spiritual body), then, becomes endowed with the "dunamis" power (internalized life transforming power which ignites change from within) and the ability to achieve necessitated soul health and stability.

As a prophet, the words that you proclaim bring life. The power of God has infused your words with the authority to call life out of dead places. They nurture (which requires periodic correction) and minister (which often demands chastisement) the soul. Your words access the spiritual grace and favor of God. The words of the prophet manifest among the people and produce the things that we desire and deserve in accordance with the plan and timing of God. Your calling requires your total surrender to the authority of God.

In all this discussion about prophets, we must answer the prevailing question, "What exactly does it mean to be a prophet?" Throughout the Old Testament, there are three distinct Hebrew/Aramaic words used to refer to prophets namely, navi (nâbîy'), ro'eh (râ'âh), and hozeh (chôzeh). Each of these words embraces and accentuates a distinctive action or responsibility in the life of the prophet. The terminology is indicative of a specific action or role taken by the prophet.

Navi – The announcer or one who proclaims (Foretells).

Ro'eh or Hozeh – The seer or one who sees (Foresees).

Qesem – The diviner or fortuneteller and one practicing witchcraft.

Although there are those who would suggest that the Bible mentions diverse types of prophets, I suggest that there are only two types of prophets – true prophets and false prophets. False prophets depend on themselves and their own agendas and are motivated by self-gratification, selfishness, and lust for popularity. Their messages lack divine authority and merit. True prophets, however, rely on the guidance of the Holy Spirit for divine revelations and for the bold authority to release the word that comes from God.

It is not a matter of who, but how God chooses to use the prophet or manifest God's self through the prophet. The prophet's purpose is one of availability and total surrender to the will of God. God is raising up an army of bold prophets to defeat the influential power and presence of spiritual darkness. Are you such a vessel?

Deuteronomy 18:18-20 (NRSV)

[18] I will raise up for them a prophet like you from among their own people; I will put my words in the mouth of the prophet, who shall speak to them everything that I command.

[19] Anyone who does not heed the words that the prophet shall speak in my name, I myself will hold accountable.

[20] But any prophet who presumes to speak in my name a word that I have not commanded the prophet to speak or who speaks in the name of other gods, that prophet shall die.'

The words used in the Hebrew text merely distinguish methods and modes of prophetic functioning. The roles, responsibilities, and actions of the prophet remain subject the plan and purpose of God. Throughout the biblical text, prophets operated and functioned differently, but their purpose remained the same, to disseminate the wisdom of God to the people. The prophet served as the messenger (navi) delivering words of correction and divine judgement upon rulers and nations. Prophets also delivered messages regarding future events and occurrences. In other instances, the prophet operated in the capacity of a seer (hozeh), as one who received divine messages through dreams and visions. Still, other seers (ro'eh) received divine insight and possessed heightened spiritual perceptions and intuitiveness concerning people and situations.

Prophets may operate in any combination of roles – messenger, visionary, and spectator – depending on what God requires and as their gift and calling become perfected through the Holy Spirit. There is, however, but one viable classification of prophets—true prophets. It is the will of God which must be accomplished through the prophetic work. How God elects to operate through a chosen vessel remains the uncompromised authority of God.

As previously shared with you, because of the work required by the office of the prophet, your life does not belong to you. Your time becomes God's time. Your plan submits to the divine plan of God for your life. Your heart must feel and sense the heart of the people and beat with the rhythm of God's Spirit. Your mouth must yield to the voice of God. Your way must align with the way in which God chooses to lead you. God will hold you accountable for the effective delivery of God's word to the people of your assignment. In fact, the very messages proceeding forth from your mouth do not belong to you. Therefore, you have not the authority to take credit for what God reveals to you or through you.

You must be willing to sacrifice of yourself and to sacrifice your whole self to the will and plan of God. Moreover, as we consider the sacrifices of this formidable calling, I admonish you to remember that the sacrifices you make for the purpose of prophetic ministry do not always merit monetary value. There are things whose value surpasses the filthy lust of money delivering satisfaction, peace, and wholeness to the soul and spirit of individuals and the collective body. Let me say it this way, the prophetic call is not the means to a greater financial end. You cannot embark upon the appointment of prophetic zealous for monetary gain, power, prestige, or position. Christ calls those in whom He sees and recognizes the value and potential which rest innately within the human vessel.

Now, let me take a moment to explain the value of you, the creation of God appointed to carry the mantle of God's prophetic authority. Diamonds and pearls are both precious and highly valued stones. People willingly pay a great price to be adorned with such precious stones. The beauty of each lies in the story of their making. While highly valued and sought after, neither of which possesses any value, nor peeps the interest of the poorest among us in their original state. Diamonds are merely lumps of dirty coal that have endured immense pressure under the weight of the earth, while pearls are formed from grains of sand trapped within the tight grips of oysters being coated in the secretions of the oyster because the oyster perceives the sand particle as foreign, unwelcomed, and undesirable. Like diamonds and pearls, the weight of your sufferings and experiences, the ostracizing, neglect, rejection, abuse, hurt, and pain you had to endure has shaped you into something more precious and more valuable than how you perceive yourself.

The words of The Christ should bring reassurance to who you are and to the calling of God in your life. The Lord sees the potential and promise that lie within and uses the circumstances of lives to shape us into the highly valued and precious vessels that will bring overwhelming glory to the Name of the Lord. Jesus said this,

Matthew 7:6 (NIV)
> Do not give dogs what is sacred; do not throw your pearls to pigs. If you do, they may trample them under their feet, and turn and tear you to pieces.

This text is just as much about you as it is about me. Stop devaluing yourself discrediting your gifts and talents to appease the insecurities and inadequacies of jealous and hateful onlookers to the glory being revealed in and through you. The times and seasons of castrating your destiny and purpose and forsaking who you must cease and desist. Just as dogs do not appreciate things of value and pigs do not see or recognize the full value of a pearl, there are people attached to you, and those who surround you, that lack the intellect and spiritual prowess to recognize or appreciate the true value of who you are in the spiritual realm.

Sever unfruitful connections. This is difficult due to the human need for association and togetherness. Stop forcing bonds, connections, friendships, relationships, and associations with people that spiritually do not mesh or fit together. The repercussions of such are costly. The truth is, not everyone around or connected to you is truly for you, nor do they care about you or the potential of your being. You have value but you must surround yourself with other individuals of esteemed value to experience the appreciation of your value. The Spirit of God bears witness to anointing on our lives and makes known those things which add to the value of your anointing. It takes the truly spiritual and anointed to fully appreciate your spiritual worth and value.

Before you can expect others to appreciate your value, you must first acknowledge the totality of who you are and the struggles that you have overcome to get where you are. All that you have been through and survived has made you into the vessel you are today. Never forget or forsake the value of you. Your value is God's value. Your life is the evidence of the power of God's love and the glory of God manifested in the world. Beloved, you are the embodiment of grace and favor.

When and if we take time to carefully consider our own pains and struggles, we will easily digress considering how great God has truly been good to us, despite the things we have done and to which we have subjected ourselves. The splendor of the Lord often overwhelms us. However, it is in the light of divine truth which we must pursue the true purpose of our divine being. God chose me, and God chose you, for this season. As the Lord chooses us, it is incumbent upon us to respond to the calling of God on our lives.

Those whom the Lord calls to the elevated office of a spiritual prognosticator, must, him/herself, choose to follow the Lord's bidding to deny themselves. Such a great sacrifice requires the relinquishing of your personal will and desires. You cannot lead if you never bleed. There will be pain. There will be sacrifices. It will not always be glorious. You will shed tears. You will face your fears. The reality is that you will surrender all to the One who has called you comforted and assured of God's faithfulness and bountiful favor dispatched to redeem and to restore you whenever the well of your own strength has been depleted.

God's will and plan have priority in the loves of those anointed to offices of spiritual leadership. It is the fulfillment of God's divine will and plan for your life which orchestrates the glory of your life's story. Glory does not come from you, now those assembled around you. The glory which dispels and shuns the evilness and darkness of this world comes from the Lord. You must be committed and resigned to God's plan to become the emulation of glory all the while recognizing that it is the power of God at work within and through you, not you.

Such sacrifices of mere individuals for the sake of the calling of God saturate the biblical story. Sacrifice remains a critical factor in the pursuit of prophetic purpose and covenant relationship. There is a plethora of stories throughout the Bible which acknowledging the extent to which those who pursued the prophetic call made sacrificial devotion. The life and calling of the prophet Jonah exemplify this. Jonah sacrificed his pride and personal prejudices and preferences to satisfy spiritual assignment and prophetic work God gave him. And like Jonah, each of us must confront our prejudices, preferences, and pride as oracles of God. The word must never return void because you were intent upon your own agenda which failed to align with the unction of God.

The people of Nineveh possessed a spirit of disobedience and defiance to the power of God. The gods they made and constructed held greater importance and influence in their lives. God had grown angry and displeased with their idolatry and blasphemy. The Spirit of God delivered unto Jonah a message of correction and rebuke for the people in this ancient Assyrian city with its waywardness and unrighteousness. Nineveh was located within the region of Upper Mesopotamia, on the outskirts of Mosul, which is in modern day northern Iraq along the Tigris River. The people of this region have historically believed and practiced faith differently, worshipping idols and abandoning faith and allegiance to the Lord God.

God directed Jonah to pronounce the destruction of this city and its inhabitants if they continued to abide in their wickedness and refused to follow faith in the One True God. Nevertheless, God commanded the prophet, Jonah, to speak against the treachery of the government, something which people today refuse to do for fear of disassociation and not being approved, affirmed, acknowledged, or accepted. Prophets of God do not thrive or survive on the approval, acceptance, acknowledgement, or affirmation of individuals. Prophets strive to please God through their obedience to the will of God.

Beloved, the prophetic calling requires fearless unyielding boldness to speak truth to the powers which rule across the land in clear defiance to the will of The Almighty. We must address spiritual wickedness in high places. Prophets avoid the pettiness of problematic people within the assembly. They earnestly seek to restore order. They are motivated by the opportunities and demands to provide spiritual direction, clarity, and guidance to the people of God for the purposes of spiritual growth and development, and the advancement of God's Kingdom in the earth.

With such a daunting task and thankless mission laid before them, prophets are called upon to sacrifice their own selfish pleasures to stand before the people as the voice of God. There are times when the prophet must stand and boldly proclaim even when the hearts and minds of the people are not focused or centered on God. Prophetic work is not for the faint at heart or the weak in spirit. Prophets must promote and proclaim the plan of God to redeem, rescue, restore, and revive, not to meddle, manipulate, or masquerade faith.

Melancholy clouds of death, doom, and destruction loomed over Nineveh. Nineveh brought utmost displeasure to God through its vast acts of spiritual impropriety, malodorous behaviors, impotent polities and protocols, religious rhetoric, and apathetic attitudes. Adversity, afflictions, distress, death, malevolence, and sadness plagued the city and its inhabitants. And although the people exhibited selfish and lustful pride, waywardness, and sought to satisfy their wanton pleasures rather than the desire to please God, Nineveh bore the burdensome weight of sinfulness, noisome pain, agony, misery, guilt, and shame.

It was to such a city and such blasphemous and spiteful people that God told Jonah to go prophesy. What a contentious assignment. To be told by God to go minister to an aggregation of people you despise and for which you have great disdain will cause deep resentment and frustration. Yes, prophets get angry with, and do not like or prefer all assignments. Nevertheless, God is yet calling this city and your city to repentance. Even though we remain consumed in our fleshly desires and overtaken by the darkness of this world, God still needs prophets to proclaim God's power. Although Nineveh was a wicked city, God still saw hope.

Consequently, the lesson we learn from Jonah is that there will be congregations of people and platforms from which you must proclaim "the acceptable year of God's favor" even though you disagree or dislike those in your audience. You are not there to be liked and you are not there to make friends. You are there on assignment. Regardless of the audience, we must proclaim the word of God without prejudice, bias, or personal judgement and condemnation. This is an area of dangerous temptation for those in ministry, particularly prophets. We must avoid interjecting our personal preferences into the messages we carry. The Lord did not send you on assignment to place your personal approval on anyone; God sent you to carry a message. Give it.

Ministry will present moments of discomfort and displeasure. If you are too comfortable with every message and every audience, check the origination of the messages you bring. The prophet must carry and wield the word of God as a two-edged sword to cut, discern, and divide right from wrong, truth from lies, righteousness from unrighteousness, moral from immoral, and good from evil. You may want to make people feel good with words of bountiful prosperity yet the conviction of God upon you demands that you boldly uproot and destroy the strongholds of evil and displeasure which have overtaken the body of Christ. You are supposed to be uncomfortable.

Jonah attempted to run for the assignment. You may choose to run from your assignment. However, your running will not delay or stop God from healing, loving, delivering, correcting, saving, or redeeming. Your dissatisfaction and discomfort with the word of God bubbling within you will not diminish the authority of God over any situation or circumstance. God's word never returns to God void, unfulfilled, or unaccomplished.

The sacrifice of your ego and desires is the greatest sacrifice you must make. The prophet is not a self-proclaimed venture. It is a divine calling and obligation which incurs consequences for our disobedience and defiance. The temptation to make the title and position about you and what you think or feel exists. However, you must resist that spirit of temptation and it will flee from you.

The prophetic journey is not haphazard or full of chaos and confusion; God does not author confusion. The work of the prophet invokes integrity, efficacy, accuracy, or relevancy. God provides clear direction and a specific assignment to the prophet. The instructions provided to every prophet are the same, only the audience and the message may differ. Prophets throughout the Bible, from the Old Covenant to the New Covenant, continued to repeat this message of obedience and submission to God regardless of the method or means by which one was called or the way the message was received. Once you remove the extra and superfluous details from each conversation, the mandate to the prophet is simply, "Go...preach...!"

The Bible admonishes us to conduct ourselves with the mind of Christ. The mind of Christ is one of humility and servanthood, not one of selfish pride, ego tripping, maliciousness, or personal prosperity gain. Christ was, first, a servant. When functioning in the capacity and office of the prophet, you must operate within that very frame of mind. Your life as a prophet, as well as your attitude, emulate Christ as you serve as the physical embodiment of divine authority. Moreover, it is imperative that you constantly bear in mind that God called you to serve this present age, not to be served. Like Christ, serve God first. As prophets of God, we are the servants of God first. We owe it to God to satisfy our callings and to strive earnestly to fulfill every assignment, to the best of our abilities, even when the message takes us out of our comfort zones. To this end, Paul declared to the Church of Galatia,

Galatians 2:20 (NIV)
> I have been crucified with Christ; it is no longer I who live, but Christ lives in me; and the life which I now live in the flesh I live by faith in the Son of God, who loved me and gave Himself for me.

The prophetic mantle is heavy. Not everyone has th, but you must bear it. The words may be hard to speak, but you must speak what God has delivered into you to speak. The prophetic voice does not concern your personal preferences, likes, or dislikes concerning the people to which you minister. What God commands you to speak should make you uneasy and uncomfortable.

Hebrews 4:12 (NIV)
> For the word of God is alive and active. Sharper than any double-edged sword, it penetrates even to dividing soul and spirit, joints, and marrow; it judges the thoughts and attitudes of the heart. Nothing in all creation is hidden from God's sight. Everything is uncovered and laid bare before the eyes of him to whom we must give account.

You are the voice of God in a turbulent world. The words that you speak are not your own and must bring conviction to the heart of the deliverer with equal authority as it does the hearts to whom it is delivered. God has called you to speak on God's behalf, not of your own authority. As the messenger of God, you must carry and release

God's message to the people, however truthful it may be, as well as carry the concerns of the people before God. In other words, prophetic ministry leaves no room for selfish pride or ambition. The word of the Lord proceeding from the mouth of the prophet was derived in the very heart of God. The word comes with an assignment to divide truth and to give life and hope.

As the prophet of God, you must die to yourself, to your own desires of grandeur and your own will, that the word of the Lord might live within and through you, predominating your very being and your ambitions.

Lord, decrease me that I may not be the image others see or seek, but you increase within me, move through me others may see and seek the You in me. Less of me and all of Thee is my earnest prayer.

Amen.

{ 8 }

Truth Must Prevail

John 16:12-15 (NIV)

[12] "I have much more to say to you, more than you can now bear. [13] But when he, the Spirit of truth, comes, he will guide you into all the truth. He will not speak on his own; he will speak only what he hears, and he will tell you what is yet to come. [14] He will glorify me because it is from me that he will receive what he will make known to you. [15] All that belongs to the Father is mine. That is why I said the Spirit will receive from me what he will make known to you."

The role of the prophet in the spiritual life of the church universal remains relevant and much needed necessity. How dare you think that your title entitles you to say, do, or live as you choose. It is not your will, but the truth of God and God's divine plan which must prevail. Your purpose is to proclaim the unadulterated truth and gospel of the Lord, and do it in God's season, not in your time. Prophetic work requires an "in-season" anointing which can only come from the Lord. True prophets are God-called, God-ordained, God-centered, and God-focused. You cannot serve as an effective and relevant prophet of God without a fresh relevant word from the Lord and daily encounters with God.

Prophets cannot operate from the pit of selfish pride and arrogance. The word which has been planted within your belly does not belong to you; it belongs to the Lord. It and you are God's divine property. You prophesy unto the Lord, not unto yourself.

The life of the word is like seed planted within the ground. The seed must undergo the germination process in which it must first die within the soil in which it has been planted before it comes to life. Fertile soil is needed to nurture every seed in this life-giving process. Once the planted seed has died and been reborn within the earth, the seed begins to grow within the cold, tight, dark earth. Eventually, it breaks through the fallowness of the earth's embrace empowered by the warm radiance of the sun.

The planted seed grows in two directions as it sheds and returns its shell within the earth. We bear witness to the process which takes place above the earth as the plant growing from the seed matures and eventually bears fruit to reproduce more of itself for others to enjoy. Yet, there is unseen growth taking place well below the surface, beneath the superficial experiences of our lives. It is the continuous growth taking place beneath the surface which enables the plant to live, grow, and be fruitful.

As the plant grows above the ground, the root system grows in the opposite direction reaching deeper and deeper within the earth. The roots of the plant grow downward attaching themselves to rocks, minerals, and other particles within the earth through which the roots find nourishment and nutrients to sustain continuous life and growth for the plant above the earth. Furthermore, as the roots reach into the earth they also serve as the foundation of sustainability for the plant keeping the plant above balanced and stable through its growth and reproduction.

For the prophet, the word of God must grow in both directions, both inside and outside, within and without. The word of God, the seed within, must grow within taking root deep within, constantly finding health sustainable elements within you on which to find and create a sense of spiritual and emotional balance for the work of ministry. The word must work within you so that you are equipped to produce something worthwhile and valued to give to others.

You cannot minister effectively when you are out of alignment or lack a sense of balance. Self-care and spiritual wellness cannot go unattended. Ministry requires your whole self to be effective and true to its purpose. Alignment comes through the Spirit. The danger of being out of alignment is the sabotage of your ministry and the discreditation of your witness. It is the will of God for your life which you must seek and pursue. We find this evident in the Gospel message as Christ struggled with the cup of destiny before him—the cross.

Mark 14:36 (ESV)

And he said, "Abba, Father, all things are possible for you. Remove this cup from me. Yet not what I will, but what you will.

Luke 22:42 (NIV)

Father, if you are willing, take this cup from me; yet not my will, but yours be done.

Balance, therefore, comes when you acknowledge and accept the awareness and truth of not only who you are but whose you are but who you have been called to be and what you have been called to do through God. You must undergo the transformation of your mind and purpose that what you must do has nothing to do with you and is not dependent upon you. God has called and chosen as an ambassador and keeper of God's word, but nothing about this endeavor is about you. You were selected and chosen but bear in mind that God could have chosen another.

Let us explore the notion of balance a bit more closely and intimately. Prophets receive spiritual secrets. In prophetic movement, God reveals and download divine secrets and plans pertaining to the people of God. Other prophets are made privy to plans and purposes pertaining to government and established leadership. However, the responsible and effective prophet must manifest balance within his/her own life. The emotional state and level of maturity of prophets is critical to the effectiveness of message delivery and the extent of prophetic reception.

Prophets must exhibit control over their own lives and affairs. The haphazardness and irresponsibility of your private life can disqualify your witness. It is hard to minister to people who see the disarray of your existence. When your life is evidently and obviously out of order, the probability and potential of you effectively proclaiming order in the lives of others diminishes. In this age of continual technological advancements and ever-increasing social media accessibility, people learn about you before they hear you. If what they have learned about you does note align with what they expect from you, they will not receive you.

Find and establish balance and boundaries for your life and in your ministry. This is not advocating that you become someone you are not, nor is this encouraging you to live a double life filled with secrecy. Rather, this is an admonishment for every spiritual leader to seek authorized help and assistance in successfully and effectively managing their own affairs. Deal with you. Own and confront your own issues honestly. The more we conceal who we are and how we feel going through life, the more trouble we will experience. You cannot continue to dress up or to cover up the truth of who you are while creating the persona of holiness and spiritual perfection. You are not perfect, and God does not expect you to be perfect. God expects us to remain continually in the process of becoming better than we have been.

The worst thing you can do to your ministry is to operate out of alignment with the will of God and to function without being in the state of balance. For a locomotive to arrive safely at its destination it must remain mounted upon the tracks which serve as its guide. Obstructions along the tracks will cause the train to derail and jumping or leaving the track causes devastation and destruction. Stay connected to your spiritual source. Your mind, emotions, and spirit must align and balance. The danger is that you become a walking timebomb of emotional and spiritual incompetence. Your issues and pains will creep into the manifestation of your ministry and delivery of your witness.

The seed must persevere. The seed must prevail. The truth of God's word must prevail the obstacles and pressures of your daunted past, your unresolved issues, your concealed secrets, your indiscretions, and your insecurities. It is the seed, the word, planted deep within you which must grow breaking through the fallow ground of your inadequacies and your brokenness. The word breaks through the toughness of your exterior to release life as a branch of hope growing eternally toward the light of God's presence and power. It is the light of God's presence towards which hope persists and grows despite the obstacles, objections, and deterrents it may encounter.

Nevertheless, as hope grows toward God producing the fruit of the power of God's word, the word dwells and grows within. Its roots continually growing within you, reaching to the farthest extent of your being seeking sources of strength and nourishment to balance and ground you as power and strength continue to grow within you and as life proceeds forth through you. God is working within you that life and hope will come through you.

But, be not deceived, God is not mocked, and the word of God is not to be compromised. When the roots of any plant become subject or exposed to contamination within the soil, the seed will die an irreversible death. Dead seed yields a decay of the fruit it produces and the eminent death of the plant. Guard the seed within. Be watchful of what is consumed through your mind, heart, and spirit. Just as a plant cannot be nourished by all sources of water or within earth lacking quality and substance, you cannot subject the anointing of God planted within you to any all manner of ministry. You must be rooted in ministry which exudes and exemplifies the love and power of God bearing evidence of the fruit of God's Spirit,

Galatians 5:22-26 (NIV)

> But the fruit of the Spirit is love, joy, peace, forbearance, kindness, goodness, faithfulness, gentleness, and self-control. Against such things there is no law. Those who belong to Christ Jesus have crucified the flesh with its passions and desires. Since we live by the Spirit, let us keep in step with the Spirit. Let us not become conceited, provoking, and envying each other.

The word of God is truth. It is divine truth. It is the revelation of the mind and heart of God in present predicaments, circumstances, and situations. It provides hope in midst of hopelessness, life in midst of death, and hope in midst of impossibility. The word of God in the mouth of the prophet can never be hostage to doctrinal polity, prestige, or positions. The word must live and prevail beyond our differences to establish spiritual balance between God and God's creation.

You are the mouthpiece, the oracle, of God. You are called to proclaim the wisdom and mercy of God as God has dictated and orated. Be careful. Know the difference between the prophetic work of God and the efforts of fortunetellers and soothsayers. The word of God has an urgency of release and impartation upon the lives of the people to whom it has been directed, it is not subject to personal profit and monetary gain. We do not prophesy in the Name of the Lord as a fundraising opportunity. We are called and receive unction through the Holy Spirit to release God's message to bring life to whom, when, and where it is necessary and needed and for whatever purpose God deems.

9

Speak What is Spoken

1 Peter 4:7-11 (NIV)

[7] The end of all things is near. Therefore be alert and of sober mind so that you may pray. [8] Above all, love each other deeply, because love covers over a multitude of sins. [9] Offer hospitality to one another without grumbling. [10] Each of you should use whatever gift you have received to serve others, as faithful stewards of God's grace in its various forms. [11] If anyone speaks, they should do so as one who speaks the very words of God. If anyone serves, they should do so with the strength God provides, so that in all things God may be praised through Jesus Christ. To him be the glory and the power for ever and ever. Amen.

Knowing what to speak is equally as important as knowing when to speak. Prophets often receive messages through various mediums, in dreams, visions, insight, and whispers, as the Holy Spirit seeks to reveal. It is expedient that prophets discern the messages revealed before they embark upon the disclosure of such revelations. The words that you speak must be spoken with clarity, assurance, and understanding as prophets are often expected to provide understanding and explanations to those to whom such sacred secrets are revealed.

You cannot share everything that you hear, feel, or see. Every revelation is not deemed appropriate for all people or audiences. Speak what is spoken into your spirit by the Holy Spirit and do not assume the right or necessity of adding to or subtracting from the revelation which has been divinely spoken. That which you are to speak must come from God and God alone. According to the Book of Acts, when the Day of Pentecost had come and the power of God descended upon the church, they spoke "as the Spirit gave them the ability." Prophesy is purposed to reveal the mysteries of God.

The challenge presented to every prophet was proclamation against reputation. The prophet's message exceeds the limited scope of good fortune, wealthy acquisitions, and prosperity. The truest of prophets must proclaim with powerful assurance even messages that may compromise their own reputation and acceptability within the communities in which they serve. Nevertheless, prophets must speak what is spoken. As God speaks, we must speak. Regardless of the audience or platform, great and small, the word of the Lord must go forth and must not be compromised to satiate our carnal desires or idiosyncrasies.

The truth about prophets and the assignments to which prophets must respond is that the work is rarely intended to please the ear. Prophets typically speak and deliver words of corrective insight concerning present of future activities and events. or the messages demand expedient adjustments in behavior to change impending outcomes. Even the favorable prophesies come with admonishment and warning to sway recipients from disobedience.

The word of the Lord is always a two-edged sword, there are two sides to every prophetic message, the blessing, and the curse. Consider the following Old Testament prophetic passage,

Deuteronomy 30:15-20 (NKJV)

^{15} "See, I have set before you today life and good, death and evil,
^{16} in that I command you today to love the Lord your God, to walk in His ways, and to keep His commandments, His

statutes, and His judgments, that you may live and multiply; and the Lord your God will bless you in the land which you go to possess.

¹⁷ But if your heart turns away so that you do not hear, and are drawn away, and worship other gods and serve them,

¹⁸ I announce to you today that you shall surely perish; you shall not prolong *your* days in the land which you cross over the Jordan to go in and possess.

¹⁹ I call heaven and earth as witnesses today against you, *that* I have set before you, that life and death, blessing and cursing; therefore, choose life, that both you and your descendants may live;

²⁰ that you may love the Lord your God, that you may obey His voice, and that you may cling to Him, for He *is* your life and the length of your days; and that you may dwell in the land which the Lord swore to your fathers, to Abraham, Isaac, and Jacob, to give them."

In as much as God blesses for our obedience, there are, likewise, consequences for our disobedience. It is the prophet who must speak and proclaim with earnest truth and holy boldness the words, the blessings of our obedience and the consequences of our disobedience. Prophets must prophesy as and what God commands, but they do not have the authority to make the choices for others. The gift of choice remains with each of us.

We can reference other familiar passages throughout the Bible which speak of the promised reward of blessings for diligent obedience to the word of God. One such passage can be found in the Old Testament Book of Deuteronomy, Chapter 28.

Deuteronomy 28: 1-2 (NKJV)
¹ "Now it shall come to pass, if you diligently obey the voice of the Lord your God, to observe carefully all His command-

ments which I command you today, that the Lord your God will set you high above all nations of the earth.

² And all these blessings shall come upon you and overtake you, because you obey the voice of the Lord your God.

This prophetic text makes it abundantly clear that the secret to accessing the blessings of the Lord depends upon our obedience to God's will and plan for our lives. Those who seek the blessings and favor of God must "diligently obey" God. According to the New Testament promise declared by Jesus in the Gospel of John, Chapter 10, the Lord has promised to reward the righteous with the abundance.

John 10:10 (NRSV)

The thief comes only to steal and kill and destroy. I came that they may have life and have it abundantly.

The Bible repeats that message of divine promises of increase, provisions, wealth, and abundance. However, blessings come with obedience to God's divine will. Consequently, those called to a life of ministry, particularly those in prophetic ministry, must live our lives in total obedience to God so that the power of God may flow freely through us and that the blessings of the Lord may gladly overtake us.

The obedience of the people first begins with obedience of the prophet. Prophets cannot live or attempt to operate in disarray, discord, or dysfunction; there must be order within the life of the prophet. Haphazard undisciplined spiritual leaders produce generations of wayward church attendees, individuals devoid of spiritual substance, conviction, dedication, devotion, discipline, or genuine desire for the things of the Spirit. As God's prophet, God's holy mouthpiece, an oracle of divine truth and authority, our lives and our witness must first be subject to the supreme will and authority of God. We all have choices to make. Prophets must choose to obey God. Choosing anything and anyone to the contrary renders prophets as false and ineffective within the Body of Christ. The disobedience of the prophet leads to death, destruction, and devastation.

Those profess to be prophets called by God who choose to function outside the boundaries of God's will and without spiritual discipline have become what the Apostle Paul described in 1 Corinthians 13, "a noisy gong or a clanging cymbal". Their witness and message lack the enthusiastic substance of a spiritual conviction and a heartfelt melody. Preaching and prophesying making senseless noise.

In fact, it behooves us to explore the Apostle Paul's text a little further. Paul's letter to the Church of Corinth is indicative of the challenges which confront spiritual leaders even to this present era. Our communities are saturated with people pleasers and pleasure seekers. Hedonism and carnal thinking dominate our modern culture in ways which early church leaders would not comprehend. The ease of access to worldly pleasures through technological advancements have established a constant presence and have become the bane of our social survival and dependence. Yet, it was to such a congregation and community that Paul composed this most significant letter.

Paul summarizes the totality of our spiritual life and attributes the fulfillment of our joys, pleasures, successes, and accomplishments to the power and authority of love. This is not either of the social, sexual, sensual, self-centered, speculative, or skeptical variations of love. Rather, Apostle Paul disrupts our thwarted and warped patterns of thinking through his reference to love in its rawest and most universally unconditional forms – agape. It is this type of love which gives utmost power to the authority of our witness and prophetic voice. Without such, we are nothing and have nothing substantial to profess, proclaim, preach, or prophesy.

1 Corinthians 13:2-13 (NRSV)

2 And if I have prophetic powers, and understand all mysteries and all knowledge, and if I have all faith, so as to remove mountains, but do not have love, I am nothing.

³ If I give away all my possessions, and if I hand over my body
   so that I may boast, but do not have love, I gain nothing.

⁴ Love is patient; love is kind; love is not envious or boastful or
   arrogant,

⁵ or rude. It does not insist on its own way; it is not irritable or
   resentful;

⁶ it does not rejoice in wrongdoing but rejoices in the truth.

⁷ It bears all things, believes all things, hopes all things, endures
   all things.

⁸ Love never ends. But as for prophecies, they will come to an
   end; as for tongues, they will cease; as for knowledge, it will
   come to an end.

⁹ For we know only in part, and we prophesy only in part;

¹⁰ but when the complete comes, the partial will come to an end.

¹¹ When I was a child, I spoke like a child, I thought like a child,
   I reasoned like a child; when I became an adult, I put an end
   to childish ways.

¹² For now we see in a mirror, dimly, but then we will see face to
   face. Now I know only in part; then I will know fully, even
   as I have been fully known.

¹³ And now faith, hope, and love abide, these three; and the
   greatest of these is love.

Pity the professed prophet attempting to prophesy without a heart
of love. Bitterness and the abandonment of self must not replace the
power of God's love. God is love and to prophesy is to declare and
proclaim God — love — to the world. If nothing else, the prophet is
obligated to spread and to proclaim God's undying and underserved
love to all.

10

The Source of Your Authority

Luke 10:16-21 (RSV)

16 "He who hears you hears me, and he who rejects you rejects me, and he who rejects me rejects him who sent me." 17 The seventy returned with joy, saying, "Lord, even the demons are subject to us in your name!" 18 And he said to them, "I saw Satan fall like lightning from heaven. 19 Behold, I have given you authority to tread upon serpents and scorpions, and over all the power of the enemy; and nothing shall hurt you. 20 Nevertheless do not rejoice in this, that the spirits are subject to you; but rejoice that your names are written in heaven." 21 In that same hour he rejoiced in the Holy Spirit and said, "I thank thee, Father, Lord of heaven and earth, that thou hast hidden these things from the wise and understanding and revealed them to babes; yea, Father, for such was thy gracious will.

The fire must burn from within. The source of your authority, the zeal of your witness, your excitement and enthusiasm for this work must come from within. The Spirit of God must abide inside of you. In the Gospel of Luke, the apostle iterates a particular Greek word for power, *dynamis*. This form of power is different from the authority which comes from a title or position; it is genuine energy and enthusiasm which resides deep within.

Luke 24:29 (NIV)

49 Behold, I send the Promise of My Father upon you; but tarry in the city of Jerusalem until you are endued with power from on high."

This power refers to inherent power or ability; it is a power than comes from deep within and explodes outward. This is the root form of the word "dynamite" an explosive mechanism which explodes from within its casing causing extensive external damage. It is this type of power which abides within us. This power is our authority. Our authority and power come from within not from our titles, offices, or positions.

We need the power of which the Apostle speaks. Beloved, the Holy Spirit abides within us to consume the very soul of every prophet with the refining fire of the Lord. If the Holy Spirit does not abide within you, you have no source of authority for the prophetic work. Such revelation comes through the Holy Spirit alone. Therefore, it behooves us to understand that the fire of the Holy Spirit remains the source of authority for prophetic ministry. Those engaged in this type of ministry have no other recourse but to rely upon the Holy Spirit for the revelatory knowledge to share. The Holy Spirit must abide within you.

More than your title, more than the vestments, more than the public recognition, this work requires much more. There is no honor or power in your title when there is no evidence of your authority. How pathetic and unprophetic the church has become when pulpits are populated with self-declared prophets who lack a true prophesy, individuals shouting cliches and ranting wishful thoughts. Shame, guilt, and turmoil now tend to overshadow the pulpits where the impotent and pointless now assemble. Prophets must yield to the Holy Spirt as the Spirit works to constantly perfect you without you ever becoming perfect. You will always be in the state of becoming, always being refined, always being made over.

Consequently, in this present age of intellectual acumen when information and knowledge are accessible in the palms of our hands, prophetic unction requires the more of us. Think about it, information is at available at our fingertips. Prophets must now be world class citizens bearing factual knowledge of the world around us inclusive of all things spiritual, carnal, social, economic, political, educational, theological, and humanitarian. The office of the prophet and prophetic work require these things of you. You must know the purpose. You must the plan. You must know the power. You must know the source.

It is one thing to declare that you have the gift of prophesy, but it is another thing to live and fulfill the purpose and plan of the one who has authorized the power which works within you. You did not call yourself to this office of spiritual leadership, nor do you possess the power of yourself to call or anoint yourself. Those called by God bear the marking of God upon their lives. There is a sweet yet savory fragrance which surrounds them as the Spirit of God rests upon them. Anything which has been touched by the hand of God bears the stain of God's presence upon their lives. It is a spiritual fragrance which emanates from within repelling the legion of hell's minions gathered around you. It is protective and powerful. It covers and caresses. It bears the authority to criticize and correct, repel, and rebuke, yet declare life to the lifeless, dispense healing to the hurting, and shatter the chains of oppressiveness thus delivering the souls of the captive.

The prophets of the Lord do not stand one the isle of their own individual authority. What empowers and emboldens the prophet is the power of God which must abide within. Every word spoken out of the mouth of the prophet during a prophetic unction must be infused with the Spirit of God. It is for and about God that the prophet proclaims, not the agenda, desires, motives, whims, or ambitions of individuals. Prophetic talk is God talk for this present age.

In Chapter 5 of the Gospel of John, Jesus explains the source of his divine authority. His authority is not self-given, but it is self-assured. You must know who called you to this work and have assurance in the power of God at work within you and believe the words that you proclaim.

John 5:19,30 (NIV)

[19] Jesus told them, "Truly, I tell all of you emphatically, the Son can do nothing on his own accord, but only what he sees the Father doing, What the Father does, the Son does likewise...[30] I can do nothing on my own accord. I judge according to what I hear, and my judgment is just, because I do not seek my own will but the will of the one who sent me.

You must confidently and assuredly stand on the knowledge of who you are in God. Likewise, you must believe that God operates and dwells within you. Jesus, in his humanity, acknowledged that he could do nothing on his own accord or within the limitations of his humanity. Jesus, our great prophet, declared his commitment to fulfilling the will of the One who sent him from eternity into time and space to be the propitiation for humanity's redemption.

Beloved, it is the will of God on which you must stand, profess, and proclaim, and no other. If you have truly been called, anointed, and appointed by God to be God's prophet then you have been to the altar of Divine presence, bathed in the blood of Lamb's sacrifice, surrendered your very being to the supreme authority of an unseen power, and had your lips purged of your own selfish and self-serving will with hot coals from the altar like the Prophet Isaiah. These coals, unlike natural coals, are heated by the eternal flame of God's divine presence, not flames of condemnation or damnation but flames of abiding love.

Until you have been purged you are not fit for the prophetic work. Purging is the process of removing that which has been deemed unwanted, undesirable, unnecessary, or useless. It requires the work of a greater element or force to rid or remove the unwanted d element. There are factions of our lives that God must purge from us; somethings about us must die in order that we may live and that others may live through the words that we speak.

To be the Prophet-King, even David understood the purpose and power of purging and submitting himself to the will of God. After yielding to the desires of his flesh and abusing his kingly authority through manipulation and the assassination of an innocent man, David surrendered his will to that of the Lord's. This small portion of David's prayer in Psalm 51 should be the desire of all who seek to do God's will and to fulfill God's purpose,

[7] Purge me with hyssop, and I will be clean.

Wash me, and I will be whiter than snow.

This is a prayer of cleansing and submission to God's supreme authority. It is an exercising in humility when you acknowledge your own flaws, failures, and imperfections, as well as the villainous and malicious intentions of your heart and surrender yourself before God's altar for scourging and purging of the dark elements of yourself.

The purging that we seek is not the purging of the charismatic church in which people with a host of their own sins, issues, and demons forced others to "purge" their sins in the presence of other church goers. Beloved, people cannot purge people. For those of us who lived through this process, where were really witnessing was mere exposure and public humiliation. Purging as a divine process in your becoming requires the move of God's Spirit. Only God can truly purge us. Purging cleanses from the innermost parts of our beings incinerating the filth and wickedness of our character, ambitions, and intentions.

Holy Spirit, burn it all away.

Now ask yourself, by whose authority do I stand? Those to whom you minister need to know by what authority you come to them. You will not have to declare it, but your witness should be a lived reality for others to see and experience.

The enemy is alive and doing well and will challenge your authority and the authority you attempt to wield. Remember, the enemy is devious and conniving, the author of lies and master of deception, and the enemy is much stronger than you are, especially if your arrogance, pride, and ignorance (all tools wickedness) convince you to believe that prophetic ministry is about you and what you give to the people. The enemy will eat you alive and you will witness your own demise.

Trust me, the enemy sees you and will try your authority. Matthew, Mark, and Luke share a common story about a man living in the tombs who tortured himself day in and day out and who instilled fear in and threatened those who came near him. According to the story, the evil spirits within the man recognized Jesus's authority and confronted Jesus by asking, "What business do we have with you, Jesus? Leave us alone!" The Apostle Paul records an incident in which the dark forces of the world were imitating the miracles and other divine works of God, making a mockery of God's prophets. There are chief demon spirits that you cannot contend with easily. Remember the text in Acts 19, not only did the evil spirit speak, but it challenged and overwhelmed a faction of vulnerable individuals,

[15] And the evil spirit answered and said, Jesus I know, and Paul I know; but who are you?

Who are you? God needs no more self-proclaimed, one-hit wonder prophets professing prophetic authority yet missing divine calling or placement. Perpetrators can be filled with spirit of Jezebel and be seduced by the apparent authority of the title causing them to operate under the influence of manipulation. There are also individuals who have a calling but are operating outside of their divine assignment and placement. They follow the crowd and speak what pleases the crowd but are not fulfilling their assignment from God. Regardless of who you are, who your spiritual parent is, your church affiliation, who you think you are, or how good people say you are, beloved, you are nothing and you are no one of great authority without the power and presence of the Lord at work within you. You must submit to the power of God.

Stop playing with power you know you do not possess, professing a spiritual anointing that you do not have. You may impress audiences of people with your façade of holy authority, but the enemy sees and knows you for who you are just the way that you are – broken, fallible, wounded, flawed, manipulative, self-serving, fake, ungrateful, and powerless. You will encounter a strong vagabond spirit that may overtake you in the ignorance of your weakness. It is not you the enemy is afraid of. It is the abiding presence of our holy God which compels the enemy, not you. You, alone, present and pose no threat the Satan unless you abide within the vine.

11

Voices in the Wilderness

Isaiah 40:3-6 (NKJV)

³ The voice of one crying in the wilderness:
"Prepare the way of the Lord;
Make straight in the desert
A highway for our God.
⁴ Every valley shall be exalted
And every mountain and hill brought low;
The crooked places shall be made straight
And the rough places smooth;
⁵ The glory of the Lord shall be revealed,
And all flesh shall see *it* together;
For the mouth of the Lord has spoken."

It is a lonely place and a desolate assignment but a needed place and a most certain calling. The wilderness is a necessary placement along the journey of life; it is a necessity in the ministry of the body of believers. The wilderness is an alone place of self-discovery. It is a journey into the deep reaches of your being which leads you to confront the issues of this experience called life. Your wilderness may not be the same as another's. Whatever and wherever your wilderness, learn the lessons needed through your experience.

Until you have been isolated and alone in the company of the Holy One, prostrate before God's glory, humbly submitted to the all-surpassing wisdom of God, you will never fully comprehend the value of the wilderness or the life of the prophet. Until you have been broken and castrated from all in which you found comfort in hiding from and concealing the anointing that lies within you, you will not be able to conceive the authority that God has placed within you. Do not be afraid of the wilderness. Do not struggle to avoid taking the sojourn into the wilderness.

The wilderness experience comes to each of us uniquely and strategically. The wilderness is where God will take you so that you can be found of God worthy to bear the weight of this glorious task and assignment in ministry. Each of us will experience the wilderness, but not in the same way. For me, the valley of the shadow of death. Grief had been my wilderness, my Patmos. This wilderness experience has become the place of my preparation for the next elevation in ministry. For Jonah it was the belly of great fish, for King David it was the pit of deep grief and sadness after returning to Ziklag. For Jesus, the wilderness confronted him with the temptations of his humanity and lead him to the Garden of Gethsemane to experience betrayal and the denial of those he loved and saved. The wilderness prepares you for the mysteries of the work which lie ahead of you. Prophets do not know how and where God shall lead of guide, nor how God will choose to use them for the Kingdom.

Beloved, God responds to the needs of God's people. God sends prophets through the land to address specific needs and the concerns of the people. We have great assurance in the knowledge that God sees us and knows all there is to know about us. God knows the number of hairs upon our heads, sees our uprising and our down sitting. Moreover, God prepares the road before us revealing God's own glory to us through the works that God does for us and through us. The revelations come to us and through us, but, often, they are for us.

God speaks even in times of calamity. The Lord will shift the dynamics of our human experiences, even those which appear to weigh heavily upon us, almost depleting us of the very hope that once carried us. Just when we need God most, God speaks. The Spirit of God, as the Holy Spirit did in the beginning of creation, continues to hover upon the face of the earth watchfully assessing the state of believers, and just in time, the Lord God moves and responds creating shockwaves throughout time and space. Those shockwaves are heard and interpreted by the prophets of God who translate and convey the messages that God has released into the atmosphere. Note how God guides and directs the life of the prophet in response to the needs of people,

Isaiah 40:1-5 (NKJV)

¹ "Comfort, yes, comfort My people!"
Says your God.
² "Speak comfort to Jerusalem, and cry out to her,
That her warfare is ended,
That her iniquity is pardoned;
For she has received from the Lord's hand
Double for all her sins."
³ The voice of one crying in the wilderness:
"Prepare the way of the Lord;
Make straight in the desert
A highway for our God.
⁴ Every valley shall be exalted
And every mountain and hill brought low;
The crooked places shall be made straight
And the rough places smooth.
⁵ The glory of the Lord shall be revealed,
And all flesh shall see *it* together;
For the mouth of the Lord has spoken."

Even while in the place of captivity and exile, the Lord speaks and releases power through the prophetic anointing of selected individuals. The role of the prophet remains undeniable as the Lord continues to speak into our lives and situations. Even in calamities and pandemics, God is yet raising up prophets to speak to the pain or our present predicaments and problems, prophets to condemn the wickedness and powers seated in the high places among us. Are we listening? Have we turned deaf ears to the prophetic voices in the land?

This text in Isaiah provides a carefully scripted blueprint for those pursuing prophetic ministry. The Prophet identified important aspects of ministry which continue to rest upon the shoulders of the prophets of God: comfort, preparation, exaltation, and revelation. Take note of this and remember it well: It is not the assignment, nor the duty, of the prophet to proclaim the excitement of chance rewards. It is, however, incumbent upon the prophet to speak to kingdoms and systems delivering words of authority which transform the hearts and psyche of people and the life and actions of those who bear witness to the words of the prophet. It is that voice crying in the wilderness of life's experiences and encounters who must bring down the idols of this world redirecting humanity back into a state of spiritual fidelity with God.

However, before those called to the prophetic office manifest the fullness of this calling, the prophet, whether male or female, must be in alignment with God's assignment for his or her life. The Holy Spirit has no respect of gender particularly as relates to fulfilling the plan of God and operating in a divine calling. God holds us to the standard, no prophet versus prophetess (which indicates a status less than the same). Regardless of gender, prophets are prophets. Gender has no bearing on the level of one's anointing from God. The prophet's life must be one of commitment, discipline, order, faith, and obedience to the will and plan of God.

Not everyone possesses the capacity to answer the call as a prophet or to serve as such. The Holy Spirit does not demon everyone worthy to walk in the office of a prophet. We know that in ministry, many are called but few are chosen to serve as God's prophet. The prophet's calling comes from God, at God's discretion. It comes to those who remain yielded to God's authority. There are things that only God can provide and there are things that only God can do. Certain things only manifest through the Spirit of God. God sends prophets to those standing in the need of that which only God can provide – living words of comfort, strength, hope, power, deliverance, and healing.

The New Testament of the Bible introduces us to a man named John, the herald of Jesus Christ. John's birth, life, and ministry focused solely on bearing witness of the "Light" which was to come into the world to redeem the world. John was birthed into promise and lived to fulfill that promise,

Luke 1:13-17 (NKJV)

¹³ But the angel said to him, "Do not be afraid, Zacharias, for your prayer is heard; and your wife Elizabeth will bear you a son, and you shall call his name John.

¹⁴ And you will have joy and gladness, and many will rejoice at his birth.

¹⁵ For he will be great in the sight of the Lord and shall drink neither wine nor strong drink. He will also be filled with the Holy Spirit, even from his mother's womb.

¹⁶ And he will turn many of the children of Israel to the Lord their God.

¹⁷ He will also go before Him in the spirit and power of Elijah, 'to turn the hearts of the fathers to the children,' and the disobedient to the wisdom of the just, to make ready a people prepared for the Lord."

The very birth of John fulfilled a divine promise. Not only did the Angel of the Lord appear to Elizabeth, John's mother, in her old age to declare his birth but the Angel of the Lord also appeared to Zacharias,

John's father, and declared to him the promise of a son, John. John's birth restored hope. It was the breaking away from silence and darkness and brought about an assurance that God still hears the prayers and cries of God's people.

Manifested in the birth of John rests the power to break the chains of silence in social justice matters and matters of faith liberation. Zacharias was made a mute for his doubt and unbelief in the promise spoken to him. His speech was not restored until the promised birth his son John happened.

John was unconventional in his approach as well as in his physical appearance. In fact, you may say that John was a radical predecessor to Jesus; he prepared the way for radically inclusive theological thought, study, and practice. John proclaimed repentance to a love-centered Jesus before Jesus had fully engaged in his earthly ministry. Yet John knew who he was and what he was placed in this life to accomplish. Knowing your purpose holds significant importance in our lives. John was fully confident in his divine purpose as the herald of Christ and not as the Christ.

Individuals mess up in ministry because we fail to master a simple lesson – be who God has created and purposed you to be. Like John, you must remain confident and have the conviction of knowing who you are. Avoid assuming the role or purpose of someone else. You are not someone else; you are you. God called and anointed you for who you are, not for whom someone else is, nor for whom others want you to be. You are you and you have a role and a purpose. As a prophet, you are the herald of God, but you are not God. Know your role. Know your purpose. Be who and what God has ordained you to be, nothing more and nothing less.

God did not reveal the complex details of the plan to John; nevertheless, John remained confident in what God sought to accomplish through Jesus, the Christ – the Anointed One. What God does in the spiritual realm remains a mystery to the created world. God, however, reveals these great mysteries to prophets whose purpose remains affixed to serving as heralds speaking only what God has spoken.

Historians have attributed the act of baptism as the crux of John's ministry. However, John's ministry consisted of more than river baptisms, eating wild honey and locust, and wearing camel fur as clothing. John's purpose was greater than what the world could conceive. Beloved, who you are in God and who you are becoming through God, exceeds the expectations of those who know you. Their insight and knowledge of you is limited but God's view laden with infinite possibilities.

Although he did not profess to be, John was indeed a prophet, he lived in accordance with his faith in God to proclaim a message of repentance and redemption that society and government would not, and not fully, embraced. John dared to do what those of us in the present-day refuse to do; he condemned and confronted social authorities for the rights and salvation of all God's people. John challenged the religious institution of his day its doctrines and ideologies, casting down the imagination and illusion of spiritual freedom and liberation by exposing the prejudices of the day with a simple sermon, "Repent, for the Kingdom of Heaven is at hand!"

John was indeed a prophet in every sense of the word and office. John's ministry was prophesied. His purpose was defined as a necessary aspect in God's plan. Beloved, there is a divine purpose for your existence in this world; you are no accident. You are the purpose of God. Reading more about John, nothing is spoken of John's upbringing or adolescence. Nevertheless, the implication from the text suggests that once John understood his assignment and purpose, John committed his life to speaking as the Lord guided and directed. He may not have embraced the title of prophet due to his spiritual conflict with the ritualistic and politically debased religious systems of his day, but John operated in the office of a prophet.

John 1:19-23 (RSV)

¹⁹ And this is the testimony of John, when the Jews sent priests and Levites from Jerusalem to ask him, "Who are you?"

²⁰ He confessed, he did not deny, but confessed, "I am not the Christ."

²¹ And they asked him, "What then? Are you Elijah?" He said, "I am not." "Are you the prophet?" And he answered, "No."

²² They said to him then, "Who are you? Let us have an answer for those who sent us. What do you say about yourself?"

²³ He said, "I am the voice of one crying in the wilderness, 'Make straight the way of the Lord,' as the prophet Isaiah said."

According to scripture, John described himself and his work by the words of the Prophet Isaiah as "the voice of one crying in the wilderness." John perceived himself as a lowly servant whose purpose was greater than he. He was simply the lone voice being heard throughout a wilderness of toxic religious practices, hypocrisy, judgement, scandal, criticism, complacency, manipulation, abuse, and spiritual infidelity. It was John whose lone voice was heard disrupting generations of cultural and social systems. John's message shook the very foundation of the government triggering the reformation of the religious systems of the world. The message of this prophet disturbed the dark forces of the world making John, and prophets to come after him, to become hell's target. John's boldness made him an enemy of darkness.

Beloved, when you are fulfilling your divine purpose as God's prophet, do not expect constant fanfare, applause, and accolades. Rather, you should know that you become a target, an enemy of the dark forces in the world. If you are truly prophesying the word of correction and redemption as God's prophet, the enemy wants nothing more than to silence you and to deter you from fulfilling your purpose. The enemy will cause you to doubt the anointing on your life and the purpose for which God has ordained you in this world. The enemy will distract you and attempt to deceive you just as he did Jesus during his wilderness trial. But you must stand, regardless of the enemy's tactics to deceive, manipulate, confuse, and instill fear, stand.

Again, the wilderness is a place of isolation. It can cause you to feel lonely and abandoned; forsaken and forgotten; useless and hopeless. However, when you understand your purpose as the prophet of God, your wilderness becomes a place of protection from the attacks of the enemy's circle. It becomes a spiritual refuge from the weight of those to whom you must minister. The wilderness is God's place of empowerment. There in the wilderness, away from everyone and everything else, separated from the distractions, the chaos, confusion, and cares of the world, there, God can secure your undivided attention and minister to you.

It is easy to see the wilderness from an immediate and carnal perspective and find everything negative and dismal to say and think about it. However, there are benefits to being in the wilderness. Remember, it is a factor of your assignment. Prophets walk alone. Even though there were schools of prophets in ancient days in which those who walked in the office of a prophet studied, prayed, and learned together to perfect their gifts, they heard the voice of the Lord on an individual basis. God gives each of us our respective assignments. Your assignment is yours, and mine is mine. Unless you learn to sacrifice the pleasures of life to submit to the will and mercy of God, you will never fulfill the office of a prophet.

Have you ever encountered someone who proclaimed to have a prophetic anointing, yet everything about that person vexed and disturbed your spirit? We cannot confuse the spirits of manipulation and pride with the anointing of the Holy Spirit. The Spirit of God must prune and strip those walking as prophets of all that is them; those things that bring them attention and popularity will be banished away. Their souls and hearts must stay in tune with the Holy Spirit so that when the Spirit speaks, they will hear it and move in the excellence of the anointing. The wilderness is where God can remove those things from you, your grandiose attitude, pride, love for other's attention, selfish agenda, the perversions of your heart, and all those other things which separate us from the will of God.

Like John, God needs more unconventional and radical vessels to fulfill the radically inclusive message and purpose of the Gospel message. The Holy Spirit empowers us and endows us with that which we need to transform the world through the prophetic ministry.

Consider Noah, one who embraced the unconventional to defy social expectations to do something radical. I believe Noah should also be counted among the prophets. This prophet heard the Lord say it was going to rain, preached about the coming of rain, and obeyed God's directive to build an arc. The impending rain would cleanse the world of its evil transgressions. Beloved, it is the prophet who must stand boldly to confront the worlds troubles and evils by speaking the words God decrees with authority.

The work of the prophet is to be unconventional to transform the world through radical measures. You must confront the unlikely and speak the unexpected. The words you speak have radical authority; they transform, heal, and deliver.

While on my own personal wilderness experience, I struggled to hear God, labored to sense the very presence of the Lord. I longed to be in God's presence and to experience the exhilaration and the overwhelming fervor which defines God's presence. In all truth, God was waiting on me. My experience was for me to discover and reconnect with me. So much of my life had been vested in and defined by the love and life of loved ones who had passed away that I needed self-discovery time, time to reconnect with that which is me and love all of me. The wilderness is where prophets tend to discover their voice and distinguish the purpose of their calling.

One of the greatest texts of self-discovery is found in Psalm 119. Although Psalm 119 is the lengthiest of all the Psalms in the psalter, the Psalm possesses elements of an introspective analysis and an assessment of the dynamics of the relationship between the psalmist and the

Lord. The psalmist came to a conclusively thorough understanding of who he was as a servant of the Lord and the purpose of his struggles.

The beauty of our overcoming rests in the cognizant awareness of how and by whom we overcame. Rather than dwell on the circumstances of our situation or the confinement of our peace, victory and deliverance comes in knowing and acknowledging the move of God which delivered us from overwhelming floods and pits of our lives. We are the byproducts of a God-doing moment in which our breakthroughs and deliverances manifest because of God doing what God does on our behalf. Within context of Psalm 119, the psalmist expressed his spiritual awakening and an acknowledgement of his own flaws which led him to the pits from which the Lord delivered him

Psalm 119:65-72

⁶⁷ Before I was afflicted, I went astray,
　　But now I keep Your word.
⁶⁸ You *are* good and do good;
　　Teach me Your statutes.
⁶⁹ The proud have forged a lie against me,
　　But I will keep Your precepts with *my* whole heart.
⁷⁰ Their heart is as fat as grease,
　　But I delight in Your law.
⁷¹ *It is* good for me that I have been afflicted,
　　That I may learn Your statutes.

In this meditation, the psalmist acknowledged his own misdoings but simultaneously celebrated the goodness and mercy of the Lord. The psalmist sought direction and guidance from God and pledged his allegiance to God. However, key in this text is verse seventy-one in which the psalmist discovered and boldly declared the blessing and purpose of his afflictions, "It is good for me that I have been afflicted."

Beloved, as you are becoming, you must find the purpose of your afflictions, the purpose for your struggle and your wilderness experience.

What you have endured has purpose, and God has the plan. God has not allowed your afflictions or struggles to boast but to further develop your ministry and to provide definitive purpose to your calling. The prophet must have a personal witness to proclaim among the people.

So much of who you are and who you are becoming is wrapped up in the experiences and the journey you have taken in life. Your crying in the wilderness is not without purpose. It may be cluttered with pain, predicaments, and problems, but it all has purpose. Your wilderness experiences have shaped you into who you have become. The isolation and solitude have strengthened your faith and renewed your sense of purpose in the world. You may have been separated from the world, but all the while you were encompassed by a cloud of witnesses, undergirded with their strength. They breathed life and hope into your very being.

Beloved, even in your stillness, God still speaks. Listen. Now speak.

Selah

Jeremiah 29:8-14 (NKJV)

⁸ For thus says the Lord of hosts, the God of Israel: Do not let your prophets and your diviners who are in your midst deceive you, nor listen to your dreams which you cause to be dreamed. ⁹ For they prophesy falsely to you in My name; I have not sent them, says the Lord. ¹⁰ For thus says the Lord: After seventy years are completed at Babylon, I will visit you and perform My good word toward you, and cause you to return to this place. ¹¹ For I know the thoughts that I think toward you, says the Lord, thoughts of peace and not of evil, to give you a future and a hope. ¹² Then you will call upon Me and go and pray to Me, and I will listen to you. ¹³ And you will seek Me and find *Me,* when you search for Me with all your heart. ¹⁴ I will be found by you, says the Lord...

Beloved, the Lord is still speaking. Who among you is listening? Which one of you is spiritually equipped and disciplined to speak on God's behalf? Do you possess what God requires of God's chosen prophets?

Consider the cost of this ministry and complexity of the work you must do as a prophet – the orator of God, a prognosticator of divine revelatory truths. Prophetic ministry, of itself, is spiritual accountability, you are accountable not only to God but to those to whom you must prophesy and minister. Most importantly, and often overlooked, you are accountable to yourself in the fulfillment of your divinely appointed purpose. This is a calling and assignment unlike other spiritual gifts and offices. The prophetic ministry anticipates your contemplation, resistance, reluctance, fear, and struggle. However, as you stop to think about the work that awaits you, rejoice in the knowledge that God has chosen you and those whom God chooses, God equips, and God provides.

The role of a prophet entails much more than revealing the mysteries of God; it is more than giving a "good" word to the people. Critical in prophetic ministry lies the beauty and awesomeness of genuine quiet time – blessed quietness, holy quietness and the assurance that occupies the deep caverns of my soul. There's great power in quietness and stillness. Quietness supplies your soul with time and opportunities to settle your spirit against the pressures, confusion, and chaos of the world; to reconnect with the atmosphere around you; to focus in on the power that abides within you.

A simple yet often misunderstood word found in the Psalms and Habakkuk – Selah. Mentioned seventy-four times in the Bible (seventy-one times in the Book of Psalms and three times in the Book of Habakkuk), the word present challenges to readers and scholars alike as they seek full understanding of biblical texts. People see and read the word as though it is an intended component of the readable biblical text. However, "Selah" is instructional and authoritative. Selah is a command. It demands immediate action. Although it is written within the context of the text, "Selah" demands an introspective assessment of one's present condition considering the content and context of the biblical text.

Both the Psalms and Habakkuk represent the beauty of ancient Hebrew poetry. Its purpose and meaning in the literary context of the biblical text remain obscure. Etymologically the word is derived from two words with liturgical and purposeful meanings. One such meaning instructs singers in harmonious fervor to raise their voices in praise.

Another meaning is to the symphonic orchestral movement of music commanding the instruments to be played louder. In either case, something is raised or heightened in joyful and purposeful movement towards something and someone greater and more transcendent. However, beyond the musical meanings of "Selah" lies a deeper liturgical meaning. Theologians ascertain that the ancient Hebrew letters for the word "Selah" represent an acronym for a Hebraic phrase found in Number 14:19 translated as a brief prophetic prayer for the mercy and grace of God, "Pardon the iniquity of this people."

What a powerfully prophetic term to embed within the biblical text. It is both obscure and intriguing. To student of the biblical text, those who hunger and thirst for righteousness, those committed to studying the text to attain approval and affirmation in prophetic witness, "Selah" is more than just an ordinary word. It is a gateway to spiritual peace and revelatory discovery.

Whether the term is used musically or to accomplish a directional or instructional purpose in the singing and playing of the hymns contained within the Psalter, "Selah" is a command, and a command demands a responsive action. Whether, or not, interpretation of the word possesses liturgical meaning for priests and prophets commanding them to utter a prayer of intercession for congregants gathered in worship as they climax through the singing of a hymn, "Selah" requires us to pause, to stop and think about it.

Selah was written at the conclusion of poetic verses adding a distinctive rhythm and the placement of intentional thought. Beloved, "Selah" is not intended to be read as a word in the context of the text, it is a command for the reader to do something impactful to your life purpose and ministry. As your encounter the word Selah, you must respond with purposeful action. Stop and think about it. Think about the meaning of the text and how it aligns with your life. Think about your next movement in the grand scheme of life and in your ministry. Think about the intentionality of your actions in relation to the workings of the Lord in your life. It means to pause amid what you are doing and reflect.

Selah.

As you pause, pausing to reflect is intentional and requires active listening skills. Reflecting will lead to listening and hearing what is being spoken. Every prophet must take intentional moments in life to reflect, to stop and think about what God is speaking. The prophet is nothing without the ability and willingness to stop and think, to listen and hear what God is speaking through time and space.

Too often, we become incumbered with the multiplicity and complexity as well as the accessibility of distractions which surround us in every aspect of our lives. I do not care how deeply profound you believe you are or how spiritual you consider yourself, all of us are subject to the distractions of life. For those of us who lived and ministered through the COVID-19 pandemic, we were forced to see how easily distracted we really were and how cumbered our lives were with the superficial when the world came to a standstill for two years. Our movement among and interactions with others were hampered and regulated by government protocols which forced us to examine carefully and critically that which held true value, merit, and importance in our lives. It even challenged us to revisit how and why we do ministry.

As the world stopped around us because of an unforeseen pandemic which claimed the lives of millions in a matter of two years, life continued to happen around us. Souls still needed ministering to. Souls still needed to be saved. Lives still needed to be changed. The Spirit of God continued hovering over the created world surveying the hearts and needs of people and speaking profoundly to the crisis of the world and the situations of life in which we found ourselves.

Nevertheless, the lessons learned were not only physical and emotional but spiritual. There is much to consider and to think about as we journey through life each day, as crises continue to assail us and as life continues to happen around us, God continues to speak.

Consider the fullness of what your life entails. Not only are you the prophet; but you have family responsibilities, you lead a congregation; you must maintain the professional duties of secular positions; you strive to remain social active and involved keeping human connections and awareness of the struggles and challenges we all must face; you are faced with confronting your own human desires and passions. You must be honest and transparent with yourself and even face your fears. *Selah.*

Every prophet must take the time to listen for and listen to God speaking. These quiet moments come in distinctive places in which the prophet can find solitude and spiritual sanctuary away from the chaos and clamoring of the world. Beloved, noisome burdens impede our ability to hear the voice of God with clarity and assurance. Prophet you must hear from God clearly and be precise in your proclamation.

Listening and hearing are critical. If your ability to listen is challenged, then your ability to prophesy is thwarted. You cannot prophesy if you do not listen. Never forget, the call to the office of a prophet is not about you; it is not the platform to promote yourself, aggrandize, or vaunt yourself above others. You are not the focus; it is the word within you that you carry, the fire in your belly. It is the message of the Lord that you have been tasked to herald which matters. Learn to listen and do just that, listen. Remain silent when it demands so. Speak when spoken into. Be still when told to. Pray because you need to. *Selah.*

Hearing is a physical sensory ability. However, listening is a required learned skill in the art of effective communication which consists of shared mutual dialogue in which one clearly articulates a message as the audience listens attentively. Truth is, one can listen to a message but fail to understand the content, meaning, or purpose of the message. Think about the sermons you have heard throughout your life. You were present and listening to the prognosticators of the Gospel, some more influential and powerful than others, but you were present, nonetheless; present but you failed to connect with the message and/or the messenger, thus listening but not hearing. Hearing is the act of intentional listening with the purpose of comprehending the message being conveyed. Consider the following as necessary requirements of hearing:

1. Be present and engaged.
2. Listen with intentionality.
3. Seek understanding.

First, hearing requires your presence. You must be present and engaged in the communication taking place, not distracted and unengaged. Your body and mind must be present to engage in the hearing process. Sometimes we may be physically present, but our minds are in a host of other places. We are engrossed in being busy chatters and tweeters but are not mentally present with those sitting before us. Every now and then, it is important to put technology away, although it is an asset in our modern world, the easy access to technology poses a hinderance to the fundamental art of communication.

Be present and engaged with those before you. Give your attention to the present, that which sits before you within your reach and grasp. Are you present, when God is speaking, or do you find yourself victimized by distractions and the temptations of the world around you? Prophet, this is a divine mandate; God needs your attention.

Second, hearing demands that you listen with intentionality. There is an adage which states, "We can all sing together, but we cannot all talk together." One aspect of healthy communication is that while one is speaking, the other refrains from talking and listens actively. Active listening requires the attentiveness of your body in the conversation. Your body must speak and convey the message, "I'm listening." It is impossible to listen to someone speaking if you are too preoccupied with doing all the talking. The same holds true in the spiritual realm; you must stop talking and complaining so much and take the time to listen to what God is speaking to you. Just stop talking. Listen.

The third element of hearing requires you to seek to extract understanding from the messages being conveyed to you. Wisdom and understanding do not come immediately. And for the prophet, you must seek and ask for both wisdom and understanding from the Lord who, alone, can supply them. Whether your prophetic journey encompasses visionary revelation through dreams, rhema utterances, or the ability to peer into divine futures, the prophetic leader must devote undisturbed time in the presence of the Holy One.

Public speaking and homiletical theories suggest that prepared messages contain a clear purpose and provide listeners with valued reasons to want to hear and to receive your message. Why would people want to hear you? What impactful, transformative, relevant word do you have to deliver to the people? What credentials do you bear to validate your title? This is not about college degrees because college degrees alone do not validate you or authenticate your message. Your validation comes through the Holy Spirit and your credentials are the evidence of your efforts. People need a reason to want to hear what you have to say. Therefore, it is critical that as you engage in the hearing process, you, too, must seek to extract elements of truthful authority and revelations of divine promise. You must want to know more and possess the need to understand what God is speaking.

Be mindful, though, it is not the prophet's responsibility to make sense of or to justify God's purpose for the prophetic message. It is the duty of the prophet to carry and clearly convey the message. Why and who God choose as the audience of prophecy is not yours to justify or approve. You are the vessel and the voice of God. God does not need your approval or affirmation.

Peculiar as you may be as the prophet leader in the Lord's Church yet chosen for this assignment of utmost responsibility and accountability despite the multiplicity of your flaws and imperfections, it behooves every prophet to know and understand your purpose in prophetic ministry. It is not a matter of first and last; we are not in a race against one another to see who releases prophecies first or the fastest, nor is it a matter of who draws the greatest crowd. This is not a popularity contest. Rather, prophetic ministry is a matter of accountability – your accountability to God.

You are responsible to God and God is holding you accountable to do and say whatever God speaks. Mutability of God's message is not yours to decide. The Lord will hold you accountable for your response and obedience to God's directive. Despite of where God sends you to speak, no matter the audience that you are directed to address, and regardless of what God speaks for you to say, go, and do. Your obedience will yield, not your reward, but will be the catalyst for change in the lives of others.

God is speaking to us today, in the church, through the church, and about the church. It is imperative that the prophets of God stop and think about that, think about what it is you have been commissioned to do and what God has assigned you to say or do. You must consider the details and depth of what God has revealed to and through you.

Think about this, God chose you just as you are, and you must embark upon this work just as you are. Be genuine in your approach and appearance and avoid the temptation of grandeur. Although this is a magnificent work and a grand mission, humility, sincerity, and genuineness of character reside at its core.

Discernment will serve as your guide along this journey of prophetic inquiry and revelation. You must know God's voice and knowing the voice of the Lord only comes through spending purposeful quality time in God's presence. The prophetic vessel not only bears the weight of the spiritual mantle, but the effective prophet must commit to a life of prayerful communion with the Spirit. You cannot expect God to speak and deposit into your spirit when you fail to devote time with God in God's presence.

Do not be that voice crying in the wilderness of life which speaks impetuously, inappropriately, inaccurately, or incorrectly in the Name of the Lord only to serve your own agenda or to inflate your ego. Do not get caught up in you. Surrender to the Spirit of the Lord and stay there – stay in God's presence, surrendered, availed, and humbled. Be the voice which embodies the presence of God so that we continue to hear God through you and see God at work in you.

God needs prophets who will listen. God needs those who not only hear the voice of the Lord but who listen as God's speaks, listen not only for what you want to hear but for that which God is speaking in season. God needs prophets who will submit and surrender to the will of God. More importantly, God needs prophets committed to the mission and focused on the vision of the Kingdom.

Be that one, the prophet of this present age, who remains aware of the movement of the Spirit throughout the world around us, that one who listens for the voice of the Lord and can discern God's voice despite the distractions which arise around you.

Beloved, listen God is speaking. Can you hear the voice of the Lord speaking within you. Are you able to silence the distractions around you?

Do not allow the prophets and the voices of those crying in the wilderness to die among us. Silencing the prophetic spirit within the church will cause further death and destruction to the church as a spiritual entity within our communities. We have remained silent far too long allowing the systems of this world to speak in our place, but God needs voices to speak for God to condemn reprobate and contrary spirits, those who will boldly and ably tear down the systems of injustice, hatred, and corruption which profane our societies and have divided the House of God until we are now warring against ourselves.

Speak what God is speaking into you as God gives it to you. Like the Blessed Mother, Mary, the Word that you carry within you will come through you but is not of you; it does not belong to you; it is not yours to hoard, keep, or manipulate. As it grows within you, you will experience great discomfort and the pain of the word you carry will cause you to push and press forward until the need to deliver and to give birth to the message within you will overwhelm you. What has been growing within you has stretched you and strengthened you in ways unfathomed. But remember, although the word in you may be for you, it does not belong to you. Release it.

Beloved, I speak a release to the prophet in you. If God has truly appointed you in this season and laid upon you the mantle of the prophet, walk boldly in your divine calling and appointment. Stand up. Speak up. Remain prayed up.

Selah.

{ 13 }

The Prophet's Prayer

2 Chronicles 6:18-21 (NKJV)

[18] "But will God indeed dwell with people on the earth? Behold, heaven and the heaven of heavens cannot contain You. How much less this temple which I have built! [19] Yet regard the prayer of Your servant and his supplication, O Lord my God, and listen to the cry and the prayer which Your servant is praying before You: [20] that Your eyes may be open toward this temple day and night, toward the place where *You* said *You would* put Your name, that You may hear the prayer which Your servant makes toward this place. [21] And may You hear the supplications of Your servant and of Your people Israel, when they pray toward this place. Hear from heaven Your dwelling place, and when You hear, forgive.

Lord, I declare the release of Your prophet. I pray that Your servant may hear Your voice with clarity, see and discern the visions with accuracy, and speak Your word with bold assurance and authority.

Unleash the multitude of blessings upon Your servant's life. Let every need be satisfied with the abundance of Your provisions. Surround

Your servant with those who will provide strength and support when the weight and load of each assignment grows heavy.

Lord, I speak the release of the mantle of Kingdom authority to fall upon the shoulders of this Your chosen vessel of glory and honor. Release the magnanimous power of faith in You. May this anointing and appointment be perpetual and yield the abundance of the harvest of blessings. Rest Yourself upon this Your servant that all encountered will see and know You through the work and words of Your prophet.

Let the oil of Your anointing flow downward to drench, saturate, and sanctify Your servant as the oracle of Your righteous authority. May the words yet to be spoken bring deliverance, salvation, hope, and healing in this season and for this hour. Allow my prayerful petition and words take life, form, and action, through the Name of our Chief Prophet, Jesus, the Christ.

Almighty God, the One who remains our very present help and our hope from everlasting to everlasting, hear us. And, Lord, as Your servant surrenders to the prophet's calling, strengthen, and empower Your servant to walk in it and to live it in truth and honor of Your great name. I speak the word of supernatural release over their lives.

We speak in the power of our ancestors who bore the weight and authority of the prophetic mantle. And we seal this prayer with glad praise to the One who gives and sustains all life, the Author, and the Finisher of our Faith, the One Who Is, Was, and Is to Come, in the Name of All that is Divine. Hallelujah!

Ashé

Acknowledgement

I have labored a while with authoring this book, speaking the truth that burns within me. The innermost struggle lay not with the content of the book but with the actualization and acknowledgement of my own struggle to embrace the calling placed upon my own life. As with every sermon that I have been blessed to deliver, it remains my heartfelt prayer that what I share with others first speak and minister to me. Acknowledging the call to prophetic ministry posed a plethora of challenges for me, as I am certain it shall or has for you depending upon where you find yourself in this process.

Throughout this immense spiritual process and undertaking, the calling, and the urgency thereof, forced me to confront the flaws and inadequacies which have burdened my life. The awakening of my consciousness concerning the reality of five-fold ministry and its activation in my life revealed to me that God is not preoccupied with our flaws as God created us flaws and all. God seeks the submission of willing vessels to accomplish what God wills. It was a transformative moment when the Holy Spirit corrected my selfish thinking through the further revelation that the anointed gift of ministry residing within me was not mine to conceal. Beloved, I assure you that this is the Lord's doing and – after years of denial, running, disobedience, and suppression – it is, indeed, marvelous in my eyes.

Through the pain and sadness of the losses of multiple loved ones, it was hard to hear God. As a seasoned preacher and pastor, my heart and soul had been wounded and broken after losing loved one who were the core of who I am. Grief is lonely and painful, but God can speak even in the wilderness of our grief to heal our souls. I have never professed to be a prophet, yet I embrace the prophetic move of God through me. I have experienced it and continue to be God's vessel. I declare that God is doing something supernaturally transformative in the life of the Body of Christ.

I dedicate this work to all those, like me, who labor and have labored with their assignment. I dedicate it to those whom I love who have transitioned and to those who may find themselves now in sorrow. It is my prayer that God heal, strengthen, and deliver you and restore you from within. I also dedicate this book to those of you who may be wrestling with your calling and the assignment of prophetic ministry. May God release you to walk confidently in your purposeful assignment.

About the Author

Reverend Kenyatta R. Arnette, MDiv, PhD

The Reverend Dr. Kenyatta Arnette, is an ordained minister, an author of several Christian books. He is a bold preacher of the Gospel, a singer, an educator, and the proprietor of the KRA Ministries, LLC. He is also the Founder and Servant Leader of the Grace United Fellowship of Christian Ministries, a fellowship of networking Christian ministries. He is an avid proponent for education as the secret element to self-betterment and self-fulfillment. Dr. Arnette is the recipient of multiple awards and honors and has earned multiple degrees which include a PhD from Capella University in Educational Leadership and Administration, a MDiv from the Interdenominational Theological Center, and an MBA from Western Governs University. Dr. Arnette possesses a deep passion for Christian ministry, social justice, and unity among those he's been called to serve. Some would call him a modern-day prophetic voice of the people proclaiming the undying hope and the unconditional love of God for all people.

Printed in May 2023
by Rotomail Italia S.p.A., Vignate (MI) - Italy